FACE

FACE

A Memoir

Marcia Meier

Saddle Road Press

Face: A Memoir
© 2021 by Marcia Meier

Saddle Road Press
Ithaca, NY
saddleroadpress.com

Book design by Don Mitchell

Author photo by Cathy Armstrong

ISBN 978-1-7329521-7-1

Library of Congress Control Number: 2020943356

For anyone who has ever suffered as a Wounded Child.

And for Kendall, who fills up my heart.

"I know well what I am fleeing from but not what I am in search of."

— *Michel de Montaigne*

CONTENTS

A Red Bike

I HAD A BRAND-NEW BIKE, cherry red with chrome fenders: my first two-wheeler. Did my dad teach me to ride it? Did he run along beside me as I pedaled, holding the back of the seat until I found my balance, tipping from one side to the other, then finally discovering that middle place where you know you'll never fear tipping again? I don't remember. But I know it was a Saturday, the first day of summer vacation, because after breakfast my older sister went around the corner to her friend's house instead of to school.

The heat and humidity of a Michigan summer already gripped the day. As I went out to the garage to get my bike, I could feel my blue t-shirt grow damp and cling to my back and stomach. When summer takes hold in Michigan, moisture settles near the ground, sucking everything down with it. By late afternoon, people would be sitting immobile behind screened porches, praying for the whisper of a breeze.

Mom had shooed my brother and older sister and me out after breakfast. We lived in downtown Muskegon, where neighborhoods were arranged in blocks of small clapboard or brick-faced houses, with alleys that bisected each block. The narrow streets were lined with tall maples and oaks, which scattered acorns and, when the temperatures dipped, dropped leaves like graceful magenta and citrine flags signaling the coming winter.

Our neighborhood was filled with kids, and it was never long before a dozen or more would gather. Soon there'd be a game—hide and seek, hop scotch, tag—it didn't matter. We'd play for hours, coming home only for meals. Adults didn't worry.

My new bike had a white basket on the front handlebars and red streamers that fell from the handgrips. I had finally mastered riding on my own and was anxious to show off for my friend, Annie, who lived across the street. But on the way, I ran into Mrs. Medema, who was sweeping the sidewalk in front of her apartment building next door.

"What a beautiful bike, Marcia," she said. "And a two-wheeler! I noticed your dad was helping you balance on it. When did you take off the training wheels?"

"Yesterday!" I said, and smiled proudly. "I can ride all by myself now."

"Well, that calls for a celebration. Want to come up for some cookies and tea?"

I liked Mrs. Medema. A widow, she often babysat for us. She always wore a dress under an apron, stockings and thick black shoes. Her gray hair was cut short and curled. Three other widows lived in the brick building, but only Mrs. Medema paid any mind to us kids. She lived on the second floor, and her apartment was cozy and bright with sunshine. I parked my bike on the sidewalk in front of her steps and carefully set the kickstand. Then I walked up the narrow stairs with her, holding her hand.

The smell of freshly baked peanut butter cookies filled the apartment. My mouth watered as she took a blue-and-white ceramic plate from the cupboard and put four warm cookies on it—two for me and two for her. She reached for her blue bone china teapot above the stove, poured hot water from the kettle into it and filled a silver tea cylinder with loose Earl Grey leaves.

"We'll let it steep for just a minute," she said. "Let's go sit at the table."

She carried the teapot and the plate of cookies over to a small table near the window, then turned back to get two cups and saucers that matched the cookie plate. She placed one cloth napkin beside each cup, and poured the tea.

"Is your mom busy this morning?" she asked.

"I think so," I said, lisping. I had lost my two front teeth just a few weeks earlier. "Molly is crawling all over the place. And Chuckie keeps trying to steal my toys."

She laughed.

"Your dad at work?"

I nodded and bit into one of the cookies. My dad, my grandfather and two of my uncles owned Meier Cleaners. Dad worked every day but Sunday, when we walked four blocks to St. Joseph's for Mass and saw my grandparents and most of my aunts and uncles and cousins. After Mass the families lingered in front of the stone-faced church, catching up on the week and exchanging the latest gossip. The priest, Father Stratz, wandered through the crowd in his colorful vestments. I didn't like Father Stratz. Short and squat, he had a full head of gray hair, a thick German accent, and though he nodded and smiled at the adults, he scowled at the kids.

A slight breeze came through Mrs. Medema's screen as I bit into a cookie. I could see my friend's house across the street, and then I saw her in the front yard.

I took a sip of the tea and ate the second cookie quickly.

"Thanks, Mrs. Medema," I said through the gap in my teeth. "I have to go now."

I ran down the stairs, grabbed the handlebars of my bike and pushed up the kickstand with my toe.

At the corner, I carefully looked for cars before crossing. I started into the intersection, where there was a four-way stop. A man and woman in a tan sedan had stopped at the corner. I was halfway across the street when the car began to drive forward. I was so startled I stopped and watched. I didn't understand why he kept coming. I hunched my shoulders and turned my body to fend off the blow.

Roscoe and Muriel Benn were driving down Fourth Street in a rush. Maybe they were distracted; maybe their children and grandchildren were coming that evening to celebrate their grandson's birthday, and Muriel was anxious to get home to clean and prepare.

As they approached the stop sign at Fourth and Mason, perhaps Muriel was fussing. "Can you go a little faster, Roscoe? I still have to make the cake and get the roast ready to go into the oven. You'll have to help with the potatoes. This darn arthritis. I can't work the peeler anymore."

Roscoe pulled to a halt at the stop sign and then drove through the intersection. There was a strange scraping sound. People on the sidewalk were yelling at them. What were they saying? Muriel rolled down the window. "Stop," they were screaming. "Stop!"

Roscoe braked and the car came to a halt about halfway down the block. People were running toward them, surrounding the car. Muriel didn't understand what had happened.

"You've hit a child!" they yelled.

As Muriel and Roscoe approached the stop sign, my ten-year-old sister, Cherie, was walking home from her friend's house. Just as she turned the corner toward our house, she noticed a car driving slowly, and heard a distinct scraping noise, as if something were being dragged underneath. People on the sidewalk started to scream, "Stop! Stop!" As she watched, Cherie realized my new bike was trapped under the car. When the sedan stopped it was nearly in front of our house.

I had been dragged, caught with my bike under the car, nearly two hundred feet.

Cherie ran to the front of the car and looked underneath. I was lying on the street under the driver's side. The bike was stuck under the carriage; I was still holding the handlebars. The left side of my face was gone.

Cherie ran into our house. Mom was in the front hallway, talking on the phone with my grandmother, Mimi.

"Marcia's been hit by a car!" Cherie screamed. Mom dropped the phone and ran out to the street. My sister picked up the phone and shouted, "Marcia's been hit by a car and she's dead!" She hung up the phone and ran after Mom.

Mom's morning had begun early. Dad was gone by 6:30. Mom woke three-year-old Chuckie and baby Molly. She helped Chuckie get dressed and brush his teeth. She got a bottle for Molly, and cereal for Chuck. With four children and two adults in the house, Dad often said our cramped kitchen seemed like Grand Central Station. A large chrome table with a yellow marbled linoleum top crowded one corner, surrounded by five chrome chairs with padded yellow vinyl seats and a highchair. The cupboards were dark, the appliances spare. A small window above the sink, decorated by a frilly white lace curtain, looked out onto the side yard. Once we were all fed, Mom would send us out to play and clean up the kitchen. She was petite, though pudgy around the middle with the remnants of six pregnancies. Her dark-brown hair was clipped short and styled, and her deep-brown eyes were accented with thick, black brows. Mom put Molly down for a morning nap and started some laundry in the basement. The telephone rang. It was my grandma, Mimi, calling to check in, as she did every day. They fell into an easy conversation.

Suddenly, Mom heard people screaming outside. She was about to tell my grandmother to hold on when Cherie burst through the front door.

"Mom, Marcia's been hit by a car…"

She dropped the phone and ran to the street. As she drew near the car she saw the blood. She saw my bicycle. She felt her chest tighten, and thought, "Not again, not another one…. Dear Lord, don't let it happen again…"

By midmorning, Dad had made his rounds of the dry cleaning plant and stores and was pressing pants in a back room where one of his workers, Carl, was operating the dry cleaning machines. Hot pipes and machinery hissed and moaned. Dad was wearing shirtsleeves, but Carl was wearing a tank top already wet with perspiration. It was insufferably hot, despite the big fans droning and blowing stagnant air from above. The smell of cleaning solvents permeated the plant. When the phone rang, it was Judith, a longtime employee, who brought Dad the news.

"Bob, there's been an accident," she said. "It's Marcia. Go to Mercy. They're taking her there."

He dropped the pressed trousers and rushed through the plant, ducking automatically under the pipes and conveyer racks that hung low from the ceiling. His Ford station wagon was parked in the back alley. On the way to the hospital, all he could think was, "Please God, not another baby. Not Marcia."

What is a face? Eyes. Nose. Mouth. Cheeks. Chin. Forehead. An invitation…or a warning. A reflection… or a misrepresentation. The still surface of a deep pool…or a raging creek. Does a face really say anything about a person? Does it say everything? If a face is destroyed, does the person change? If you create a new face, do you create a new life?

When mom got out to the street, the car had been backed away. Someone had lifted the mangled bike off of me and laid it aside. Mom cradled my bleeding head until the ambulance arrived. A neighbor took Cherie and Chuck inside to comfort them and check on Molly. After the ambulance left, Mrs. Medema took her garden hose and washed the blood from the street.

I have tried to imagine my mom in those hours, drenched in my blood, holding vigil with my dad, reeling from the possibility she might lose another child to an unspeakable tragedy.

When our family physician, Dr. William Bond, saw me in the emergency room, he doubted I'd survive. My cheek was scraped off down to the bone, my left eyelid was missing, and the bottom lid was carved away from the eyeball, though the eyeball was intact. There were deep cuts and scrapes on the rest of my face and upper chest. I had lost a lot of blood. Emergency room doctors worked feverishly to stem the bleeding. They inserted intravenous lines into my arms as they tried to keep my heart rate and breathing stable enough to take me into surgery.

One of the three doctors who worked on me was a thirty-nine-year-old plastic surgeon who happened to be at Mercy when I was brought in. Dr. Bond asked him to see me as a personal favor. Dr. Richard Kislov was a brilliant surgeon who immigrated to the United States from Germany. He was known best for re-attaching severed limbs, a particularly handy skill in Western Michigan where automotive factory injuries were common. Dr. Kislov and the other doctors worked for hours, pulling skin together to fill the vast hole that had been my left cheek. They formed a bridge of skin to cover my left eye, sutured the wounds on my chest and bandaged my head. They kept me alive.

There is a place you can go, a dream state where it is easy to imagine that whatever your five senses may be telling you, whatever sounds of oxygen tanks or rustling uniforms, whatever piercings of your skin or peeling of gauze from your torn face, whatever smells of alcohol or ether, they are not real. The only true thing, in that liquid place, is the comfort of the warm encirclement of your dad's arms, the familiar drone of the box fan in the window down the hall, the slight breeze in the sticky heat, your mom's voice reassuring and deeply resonant. All reality fades into that place, and holds you suspended and safe.

Was that deep-water suspension induced? Or did the mind take over, protecting by obfuscating, by creating a separate reality? How long did I lie there, blissfully unconscious? Days, weeks—it could have been a heartbeat. But when I awoke, all that amniotic protection evaporated in the harsh whiteness of a hospital room.

I didn't know where I was. My head and eyes were wrapped in bandages, my hands tied to the sides of the bed. I did not feel any pain, but my head was heavy and I felt woozy. People around me smelled of antiseptic and starched clothing.

I was afraid.

I heard my mom's voice. She said, "We told you never to cross the street without looking."

But I did. I looked both ways.

LACERATIONS AND ABRASIONS

July 6, 1961. Surgeon's notes: Patient—a five-year-old girl—presented in the emergency room on June 17 with severe lacerations and subdermal abrasions on the left side of the face and upper chest. Primary concern was stanching blood loss and saving the left eye. Emergency closure of facial wound required pulling together tissue from both sides of the cheek. Pressure bandages applied. Loss of upper left eyelid and portion of lower left lid required fashioning of tarsorrhaphy to protect the eye.

I WAKE AND I CAN'T SEE. My face itches. My ears itch. I am desperate to scratch my ears. I can't move my arms! *Why can't I move my arms?*

My mom's voice comes to me. "It's okay, Marcia. It's for your own good."

Every day for five weeks she came to the hospital and sat by my bedside, waiting for me to wake, enduring my fearful tears when I did, watching the nurses give me shots and adjust my bandages, listening to my screams when the doctors changed the dressings. Did she retreat? Crawl into a cavernous place of denial to deal with the grief, the pain? Did she grieve? Did she feel pain?

21

Mrs. Medema and several neighborhood girls took turns babysitting the other kids while she was at the hospital. At the end of the day, Mom would go home to her three other children. Friends and family members helped out. Still, how could it have been for her to watch me cry, bloodied and bandaged, terrified, suffering, knowing there was nothing she could do but try to quiet me? Then to go home to three young children who also needed her attention. I believe she was overwhelmed, emotionally and physically.

But day after day, she came and sat. Knitting, absently crossing needle over needle, moving the yarn from left to right, right to left. I see her deft hands, her pointer fingers crisscrossing each other with each stitch, her mouth a set line, her brow furrowed. The ball of yarn unfurling.

I think she shut down. She sat and patted my hand as they pulled stitches from my face, or jabbed another needle into my arm, or held me down for another change of dressings. But she was gone. This third tragedy was more than she could bear.

His name was Patrick—their second-born, Ricky for short. Cherie was two and Ricky eight months when my parents were invited to go away with another couple for a weekend of sailing. Their friends Barb and Harvey offered to take care of the kids. When they dropped them off, my mom was fretting. She wanted Barb to make sure Cherie had her blankie at night, that Ricky got his bottle at five and again just before bed.

That night, Barb set up a vaporizer near Ricky's crib so he could breathe easier. Sometime in the middle of the night, he pulled the cord and the vaporizer over into the bed, scalding his body with boiling water. The Nedeaus raced Ricky to the hospital. My parents rushed home. Ricky died two days later.

A year and a half later, my mom was expecting again.

It was winter and the streets were icy. My grandmother was driving with mom and Cherie, heading downtown to shop. As she negotiated the slippery streets, she noticed a large spider above her head on the visor. It dropped down near her face. She swatted at it, and as she did the wheel turned to the right and the car left the road. As Cherie was knocked around in the back seat, the car ran up the guy wire of a telephone pole and overturned. Mom was thrown out of the car. Cherie and my grandma were unhurt, but Mom suffered skull fractures and ended up in the hospital for several weeks. She hemorrhaged through the rest of the pregnancy. The baby, Robert, was born several months later, but died within hours.

The boys are buried together in the Muskegon Catholic Cemetery.

Before I was released on July 23, my mom and dad sat Cherie and Chuck down in the living room.

"Marcia is coming home this afternoon, and she looks different than she did," my mom explained. "You shouldn't be afraid when you see her. She's still your sister. She's still the same Marcia."

But I wasn't.

I looked grotesque. A thick fleshy string connected my upper and lower eyelids. There was a gaping hole underneath my left eye where the skin had been torn away. A red ridge of scar tissue ran the length of my left cheek, with thinner spines spreading out like a spider web toward my nose and ear. A jagged pink scar jutted down from my lower lip toward my chin.

Chuckie was so little, only three. But Cherie was ten. She knew how I had looked, and she had seen me on the street, my face torn away. She remembers that Mom told her she would have to help a lot, because I would need a lot of care. But she doesn't recall being surprised or shocked at my face.

"I think I was sad," Cherie said, "and I was prepared to help with whatever Mom needed."

When my sister told me this, I was struck by the directive. There was an instruction in the explanation: *You will have to help. Your needs no longer matter. This accident—this tragedy— has shifted your role from sibling to responsible eldest daughter now.*

Her job was to help the family by doing Mom's bidding—to grow up before her time. And she took it on without question. She became the dutiful daughter who took over for Mom when she wasn't there, who cared for her younger siblings as needed, cleaned the house, and cooked when necessary.

She was only ten years old. An old man's inattention not only stole my childhood, but hers as well.

A few weeks after I came home, we went shopping downtown.

Mom didn't take us downtown often. It meant putting Molly into a stroller and tethering Chuck to it with a harness. I was allowed to walk freely, but in the past I had liked to go off exploring when mom wasn't looking. That often led to frantic searches and stern scoldings once she found me. But off we went.

We were in Hardy-Herpolsheimers, then the nicest department store in Muskegon. Mom was looking at some dresses and I was playing in the racks nearby. A woman came around one of the displays with her two children and stopped short.

"Oh, my God," I heard her say. She turned and pulled her children away. "Kids, don't look at that little girl."

My mom didn't say anything, just pulled my head in close to her and held me there, in the middle of the store. We left then, without buying anything, and walked home.

Now that I am a mother, I admire her ability to withstand it all. I look at photographs of myself after the accident, and think, could I have done what she did? How did she feel, knowing her daughter would probably be disfigured for her entire life?

Did part of her wish I had died, escaping the cruelty, the stares, the laughter, the pointing?

She had already lost two babies. When she was alone with her thoughts, when she kneeled beside her bed to pray every night, what did she pray for? Did she think every time she looked at me that she had somehow failed? Did she resent the care and attention I required, the money they had to spend on surgeries and doctors' bills, the time she was forced to spend at my hospital bedside? Did my swollen and disfigured face anger her? Embarrass her? Shame her?

Everything I have written here is true, but with the exception of waking up in the hospital and hearing my mother's words, I do not remember any of it.

Most of it came to me through family lore. Some of it I verified or modified after reading newspaper accounts of the accident and the days following. Some of it came from my sister Cherie. Very little came from my mother. Years later when I asked, she would not—or could not—go back to that time to help me understand.

BEACHES

I WALK ON THE BEACHES in Santa Barbara almost every day, watching the tides come in and go out. They change the landscape from one day to the next. Some days the beach is thick with sand stretching from the shoreline to the cliffs. On other days the sand is washed away, exposing barnacle-encrusted rocks, sea anemones and an occasional starfish. My Australian shepherd frolics in the waves and plays with the other dogs on the beach. And I think, How is the self built? Like the changing beachscape, we are shaped and formed by forces outside of us. Surely the self is altered by experiences, by perceptions created out of circumstance. What happens to the self if face and body are transfigured by happenstance? If that self is in early formation, a child of five for example, the self may be deeply, radically affected.

After the accident, my identity became that of a scarred child, a person whose face repulsed people. It wasn't long before I knew myself as someone to be avoided, knew that my face was frightening, even for adults. Still today, I struggle.

But little by little, I am becoming who I was meant to be.

It is 2006. I am sitting on a white overstuffed couch in the Santa Barbara office of a therapist a friend recommended. South-facing windows let in filtered light from the late morning sun. Japanese paintings hang on the cream-colored walls, creating a sense of serenity and intimacy. A box of tissues is tucked behind the lamp on the side table, within easy reach. Michael sits in a straight chair in front of me, his legs tucked under. His square, tanned face framed by waves of dark curls. We are talking about self-esteem.

"I don't have a problem with self-esteem."

"Yes, you do," Michael says.

I am stunned. "No, I don't."

"Yes, you do," he repeats, more emphatically.

I look out the window at the jacarandas in bloom, their graceful purple clusters nudged by a gentle offshore breeze.

I'd come to think of myself as confident, secure in my self-image, strong and independent. I had been a successful journalist, editor of the editorial pages of a medium-sized daily newspaper and a recognized leader in the community. I did not lack confidence in my abilities.

But that wasn't what Michael was talking about.

When I first went to Michael for help, it was because I suspected—and feared—my marriage of twenty-four years was over. After a month of weekly meetings, he suggested joint counseling with my husband. But after nearly six months, we were making little, if any, progress. So we stopped, and I returned to individual sessions with Michael.

Now here I was, sitting in Michael's office wondering what had gone wrong. With my marriage. With my career. With my life.

"Talk to me about your scars," Michael said.

"What do you mean?"

"How did you get them?"

I shrugged. Gave the rote response, something I had spent years perfecting: "I was hit by a car when I was five. I was nearly killed and lost my cheek and my eyelid. I underwent twenty surgeries over the next fifteen years."

"How do you feel about that?"

How did I feel? I didn't feel. I hadn't *felt* about it in years. I hadn't *thought* about it in years. But the more Michael and I talked, the more the memories flooded back.

"I'm so proud of you," my father says as we sit together on my bed one morning a few weeks before my wedding. He and Mom are visiting me in Redding. "Now you're getting married, I guess it's time I gave you this."

He holds out a thick, faded, dark-blue folder.

"What is it?"

I open the folder and see dozens of hospital invoices, insurance documents and doctors' bills dating from the 1960s and '70s and all carefully marked "paid" in his distinctive hand.

"Oh my gosh, Dad."

He had saved and noted each bill, each surgical procedure, each hospital stay.

As I leaf through, I come across a yellowed envelope and open it. And I see the photographs for the first time. I look for only a terrible moment, then shove them back into the envelope and put it back in the blue folder.

There is an awkward silence.

Why had he saved all these things? And why is it important to give them to me now?

Finally, I mumble, "Thanks, Dad."

He pats my leg and stands to go.

I sit alone for a few minutes, confused and overwhelmed, as if he has shown me a film clip from my childhood, one I hadn't expected and didn't want to see.

Then I walk over to the dresser and put the folder in the bottom drawer, under some old jeans. I gather my purse and my shopping list for the wedding and walk out to the kitchen where Mom is just finishing putting away the breakfast dishes.

"Ready to go?" she asks. I nod, and as we leave, I put the folder out of my mind.

Twenty-four years later, I sat on the concrete floor of a rented storage space and leafed through the files. I was instantly taken back to childhood, to when I was five. My hands shook as I sifted through the papers. And then I saw them.

The photos were close-ups, taken a few months after the accident. The left side of my face was red and raw, with ridges of skin built up in the middle of the left cheek like the spine of a mountain range. A piece of thick skin bisected the left eye, connecting the top and lower lids.

Had my dad looked at the photos before he gave me the folder? Did he consider how it would make me feel to look at them then? Or had he just put them out of his mind and not realized the impact they would have on me?

Maybe to him they were not so horrifying. He had never reacted to my face as if it disgusted him, or to me as if I were a burden. Perhaps this was his way of giving me back a part of my life that he felt belonged to me. Perhaps he was saying that I had to be the keeper of my story now, and all its attendant heartaches. Today, I believe he was giving me a gift, the gift of my past—even though I didn't want to look at it then, didn't intend to look at it ever. Now I see it as a gift of great love. Though I didn't realize that until after he was gone.

As I sat on the concrete floor of the storage unit, I stared at that child's face and let the tears come. Great heaving sobs wracked my lungs and ribcage. It was as if those pictures had the power to hold me hostage—as they *had* held me hostage for forty-five years. And I was reduced to a quivering, terrified child once again.

A few days later I took the photos out again. I could barely stand to look at them. They represented all the hurt, all the taunts, all the pain I had spent years stuffing away, convinced if I didn't think about the accident and how it made me look, it couldn't hurt me anymore.

I lowered myself to the floor. I wanted to be as close to the ground as possible; I feared I might collapse. I peered at the first photo. It was taken from the front, and that little girl was staring straight at the photographer. Her eyes were those of an old soul, someone who has suffered and survived. There was something in the eyes of that five-year-old child that was way beyond her years. Way beyond the pain and suffering, beyond the here and now, planted firmly in the Divine. Sure of who she was and sure she would survive, no matter what. The second photo, taken from the left side, was entirely different. It was of a small child, terrified—terrified of being hurt, of being abandoned to the nurses and doctors once again, of being left in the hands of people who didn't care. That child's eyes reflected such deep sadness, a grief so profound I wanted to hold her, reach out across the years and make her safe.

But I couldn't. Not yet.

TALLY

Week of 6/17/61

C. Jeanne Roslanic, special nurse 7 nights	$126.00
Ruth Fairris, special nurse 7 days	$88.50
Mildred Tayor, special nurse 7 days	$126.00
Ambulance	$12.00
Clothes ruined, undershirt, t-shirt, shorts and pantie	$5.00
Mrs. Henry Medema, caring for children	$10.00
Carol Black, caring for children	$5.00
Kathy Wirkutis, caring for children	$6.00
Housecleaning	$5.00
Total	$384.00

Week of 6/24/61

C. Jeanne Roslanic, special nurse 4 nights	$72.00
Mildred Tayor, special nurse 3 days	$54.00
Ruth Fairris, special nurse 4 days	$54.00
Mrs. Medema, caring for children	$10.00
Carol Black, caring for children	$6.00
Kathy Wirkutis, caring for children	$7.00

Housecleaning	$7.00
Total	$210.00

Week of 7/1/61

C. Jeanne Roslanic, special nurse 3 nights	$54.00
Mrs. McMann, special nurse 1 day	$18.00
Mrs. Medema, caring for children	$10.00
Carol Black, caring for children	$2.00
Kathy Wirkutis, caring for children	$4.00
Patty Wirkutis, caring for children	$1.50
Geraldine Green, caring for children	$3.00
Housecleaning	$5.00
Total	$97.50

Week of 7/8/61

C. Jeanne Roslanic, special nurse 3 nights	$54.00
Mrs. Medema, caring for children	$15.00
Carol Black, caring for children	$4.50
Kathy Wirkutis, caring for children	$2.50
Patty Wirkutis, caring for children	$1.75
Barbara Green, caring for children	$1.50
Total	$79.25

Week of 7/15/61

Patty Wirkutis, caring for children	$13.00
Kathy Wirkutis, caring for children	$2.50
Geraldine Green, caring for children	$0.75

Carol Black, caring for children	$3.00
Total	$19.25

Discharged from Hospital 7/22/61

Dr. Kislov	$650.00
Dr. Crawford	$195.00
Dr. Bond	$150.00
Dr. Askam	$65.00
Dr. Smith	$105.00
Hospital Expense	$1,302.92

Grand total	$3,257.92
John Hancock Insurance paid Hospital	$834.94
John Hancock Insurance paid Surgery	$336.50
Total cost	$2,086.48

Dressing Change

July 11, 1961 — Surgeon's notes: Dressing change is done under anesthesia to reduce trauma to the patient.

I AM LYING IN MY HOSPITAL CRIB. Dr. Kislov and several nurses surround me, and the doctor is peeling away the dressing on my cheek and eyelid. Gauze sticks to my cheek. He pries it, loosening it with water, slowly pulling it away, millimeter by millimeter. My skin holds tight. I want to cry, but the nurses hold my arms close to my chest and one says: "It's okay. It's okay. Stay still, stay very still."

I do not want to stay still. I want to push them away from my face. But the nurses hold me tight. I cannot move. So I cry. But I cry with my mouth closed, my lips pursed and my breath held, because that is the way Dr. Kislov wants it. He is the surgeon, the chief revisionist, and I have no say in this restoration project.

When I found Dad's list, I thought, *This is so like my dad.* Meticulous, careful to record every expense and include everything, down to my blood-soaked panties. Oddly, one thing is glaringly missing: my mangled bicycle. I can't imagine that he would leave that off. Maybe some kind soul got rid of it so my parents wouldn't have to confront it, and he just overlooked it when he was making his tally. Perhaps the police impounded it. Perhaps it was just too painful to consider. I don't know. But today I wonder about it. Did he somehow weigh the cost against the emotional toll? Did ignoring the bike somehow allow him to cope? I don't think he would have blamed himself. That wasn't like my dad.

The amount my parents had to pay just for that first hospitalization—$2,086.48—was the equivalent of more than $345,000 in today's dollars. It was a lot of money. They struggled to pay the hospital bills, despite the insurance payments.

Fortunately, the dry cleaning plant offered a steady—and over time, growing—income. Even so, with four children to feed, mounting medical bills were a burden. Perhaps, in intimate moments, my mom and dad talked about how they would make it through. How they would pay for the Catholic education they wanted for all their children, the uniforms, the schoolbooks.

Mom sewed many of our clothes, and Molly and I always wore hand-me-downs. Dad worked six days a week and Mom, who had an English degree, substituted at St. Joe's to make extra money. I was oblivious to much of it. But as I got older, though no one ever said it, I began to understand at some level that the financial struggle was because of me.

I have found it difficult to bring my dad to the page. Memory is a fluid thing. It moves and undulates and morphs with time. I knew him so well, knew he loved jelly beans and golf, that his Catholic faith formed him and sustained him, that he loved my mother. That he loved me. That indeed, his love may be the reason I was able to overcome the trauma I experienced throughout my childhood. But in this writing, I have struggled to find the words to describe how much he meant to me.

Often my memory—my psyche—doesn't want to go there. It's too painful, like all the hospitalizations and surgeries. I couldn't have remembered those without the notes from my surgeon. Which time was I made to lie naked in a hospital crib under a large oxygen tent? Which time did I awake and believe I was somewhere unknown, not in the hospital, which frightened me to the point the nurses had to get permission to lift a corner of one of the bandages on my eyes so I could see? Which times was I made to lie for hours, my arms strapped to the bed, as plasma dripped into my veins?

We strive to create a narrative of our lives that makes sense, and when events don't make sense, don't fall along the story line, we make things up. I am sure I am guilty of that. But the individual events I write about here are as concrete and vivid as if I were living them today. The memories just as jagged and piercing, just as white-hot with emotion, as if seared inside me by grief.

I wonder sometimes how long trauma lingers. I spent many years stuffing it into a very deep place, thinking if I did it would no longer hurt me. I was wrong. Excavating that past has been devastating. But also clarifying, opening—my chest feels cracked open.

How I miss my dad, and wish he could be here to see his daughter step into her life, finally, authentically. Terrifyingly.

I am sitting next to him at the Optimist Club's annual Father-Daughter Dinner. Long rows of tables are set with dishes and glassware, and everyone seems to know my dad, wants to shake his hand and say hello. I am so proud to be his daughter. After dinner, the men stand up and sing to us, all the old standards like "Tea for Two," and show tunes like "Surrey With the Fringe on Top," and "Oh, What a Beautiful Morning."

No one says it, no one shows it, that my face is disfigured, like a wax figure whose face is melted, whose eye is wilted. I am with my dad, who loves me, and those men, who acknowledge through their actions and their unspoken understanding they know: I could be anyone's child. Thank God for these good men, who held my dad in love and respect, who held me in a place of acceptance—for my dad, and for me.

While Mom was with me through the surgeries, a flesh-and-blood ghost, he was always in the background, an assurance and unconditional love that comforted and held me in a safe space. I don't have any explicit memories of my dad visiting me in the hospital, though I know he did. The nurses were on a first-name basis with him.

Perhaps he came in the evenings after work, to spell Mom. Or he might have come in the afternoons as I dozed. I don't remember.

When I was a pre-teen, Dad and I used to watch old John Wayne movies together. We loved Westerns. Cowboys and Indians, the good guys and the bad. Nothing was ever in doubt in those movies. You knew who was going to prevail, and even though the hero would get into a terrible fix, he always figured out a way to overcome. In many ways those movies probably fed my optimism, an optimism I inherited from my father. When we sat and watched together, I shared with him a world in which I would be okay.

When my daughter was small and I was working full-time, she went to their house twice a week, and Dad was the one who spent time with her. They roughhoused on the floor, and played "I got your nose!" They drove to Tucker's Grove Park or walked the bike path out toward the ocean. After he died, she refused to go to the cemetery or any of the places they went together. It was too painful.

My dad was the only one who made me feel like *Marcia,* not the scarred child, but the bright spirit I knew dwelled within. There is a photograph of me taken probably a week or two before the accident. In it I am standing next to my older sister, leaning in toward her with my hands on my hips, smiling as if I had just gotten away with something really naughty. That is the Marcia my dad knew and loved unconditionally. That is the Marcia I lost.

When he died, I felt like someone blasted the rock I stood upon to smithereens, like the world had suddenly turned from safe to perilous, and I didn't know how to find solid footing.

On the day of his funeral, friends and family gathered at the Catholic parish where Mom and Dad belonged for nearly thirty years. A couple of days earlier Mom and I had met with the parish priest, who said he would do the service though he didn't really know my dad. I wanted to do the eulogy, and the priest kept trying to dissuade me. Finally I prevailed. But that morning, I wasn't sure I could stand and talk about him without falling apart. I remember asking him to be with me and give me strength, and when I stood to go up to the lectern to speak, I found a sense of purpose and calm I hadn't before. I talked about how much he'd meant to me, how much he'd given me, and how grateful I was for him, and for Mom, through all those years of surgeries.

But in the years following my dad's death, I was at a loss to understand my mom's coldness and distance. Why was she so quiet? Why did she answer my questions with single-word answers, with shrugs? I wondered what I should have been doing for her, what I was lacking. She was so happy with my sisters and my brother, silent and strained with me.

Had she always been that way with me? Had it been covered up by my father's warmth?

Michael suggested she might be jealous of my relationship with Dad.

No mother would feel that way, I protested, would she? Even now as I write this it sounds inconceivable. But ....

I think about the way she removed herself when I was with Dad—disappeared to knit in the den, or headed upstairs while we watched TV downstairs.

My parents married in 1948, twenty-somethings full of confidence as the nation was recovering from war and creating a future of possibility. He joined the family business; she was teaching English at a local junior high. They settled into a small house—purchased from my dad's parents —in 1949. Cherie was born in September 1950, followed shortly by Ricky and Robert, the two boys they lost. I was born at Mercy Hospital on Christmas Eve 1955. My brother Chuck followed in September 1957, and then my youngest sister, Molly, in September 1960.

Our house had two stories, with gray clapboard siding and a long, glass-fronted porch that stretched the width of the house. The front door opened into a small vestibule where winter boots and coats were stored. A stairway to the left and just inside the front door went up to the second story, where we had a bathroom and three bedrooms.

In the front hallway was the little telephone table where my mom was sitting when I was hit. The living room off to the right stretched almost the entire length of the house and opened into both the front hallway and the dining room, between the hallway and the kitchen at the back of the house. Flocked wallpaper in crimson and black lined the dining room walls, and the living room had beige carpeting and bland walls. There was a blond console TV against one wall. I watched the assassination of President Kennedy on that TV, and Neil Armstrong's moonwalk, and swooned when the The Beatles first appeared on "The Ed Sullivan Show."

Off the kitchen were stairs leading to the back door on the alley and then down to the basement. It was damp and dark there. Shelves held dozens of canned goods and storage boxes, and there was a washer and dryer against one block wall. A tiny window high above the laundry let in a small bit of natural light, and a bare overhead bulb hung from the ceiling.

I saw my mom cry for the first time in the basement. She was sitting on a small chair among the laundry, and I had crept halfway down the stairs to see where she was. Then I realized she was weeping. I knew it was because of me, because of all the pain I'd caused her and the family. And I didn't know how to make it better, to make her happy again. So I just sat there, watching her from the darkened stairs.

I keep coming back to the basement. Monsters and ghosts, and my mother weeping. Once there was a tornado warning. I was seven or eight. Tornados were not uncommon in Michigan, but this one was serious enough that my dad came home from work. He made us all go down into the basement, Mom, Cherie, me, Chuck and Molly. But he stood near the back steps and stared out the kitchen window. At one point I crept up the stairs, wanting to be near him, worried for him. He sent me back down to the basement.

So I sat with Mom, anxious and fretting. I am trying to put myself back in that space, trying to remember how she was. I was so worried about Dad, I didn't notice her demeanor. Perhaps she tried to soothe us. Was she holding Molly on her lap? Was Chuckie clinging to her side? I remember that I would not be mollified. I was certain Dad would be taken, pulled out the window by the tornado, and I would never see him again.

ASSESSMENT

July 21, 1961 — Surgeon's notes: Surgery to assess extent of injury and healing to date. Patient's cheek and eye are stabilized enough to send her home. Additional surgery to be scheduled for the fall.

THAT SUMMER WE SPENT a lot of time at my grandmother's cottage on Lake Michigan. It was a cozy place, with an expansive view of Lake Michigan. Every year in April or May, my grandparents, parents and uncle "opened" the cottage for the summer. They took down the heavy wooden storm shutters that covered all the windows and aired everything out.

It would have been imprudent to try to spend a winter there. Snowstorms were too severe, especially at the lake, where cold blasts froze the shoreline into icebergs that often stretched half a mile out.

During the summers we spent hours swimming in the lake and running up and down the sand dunes. My grandma ruled the roost, fussing over meals and meting out discipline when needed. We often spent the nights there, and in the evenings my dad would challenge us all to an evening swim, tossing us over his shoulders into the water and letting us swim between his legs.

A large plate-glass window stretched across the front of the cottage. The expansive view took in all the majesty of Lake

Michigan, from its glittery thundering waves in springtime to the cloud-covered buildup of icebergs along the shore in winter. The main room was furnished in wicker and bamboo furniture with brightly colored cushions. The whole interior was paneled in pine. On one side of the room a large wooden cupboard held multi-colored Fiestaware: plates, bowls and cups, salt and pepper shakers, pitchers. The bright colors made meals at the cottage seem like a perpetual celebration. There was a dining room table near the kitchen, a tiny space that looked onto a sun porch where we often had breakfast. There were big shutters over the sun porch screens, and it took the strength of an adult to pull the chains to open them. The chill morning breezes would flood the porch along with the sun.

I was only eight when my grandpa died. He went to sleep one night at the cottage and never woke up. I have few memories of him, but one of the most vivid is the time a bat flew down the chimney and alighted upon the back of a wicker chair in the screened-in porch. Amid our excited squeals, my grandmother ushered all of us into the main room in the cottage and shut the glass doors as my grandpa put on leather gloves and went out to the porch. We pressed our faces against the glass and watched. I held my breath as he gently pried the tiny creature from the back of the chair. It resisted, opening and flapping its wings even as Grandpa closed his leathered hands around it. I could feel my heart beating hard as I watched him walk to the side door and release the bat to the darkened sky.

"This is Marcia," Miss Black says.

I am standing next to her chair and all the children are sitting on the floor in front of us. She has her arm around me, and I feel safe.

"Her face looks like this because she was in a bad car accident."

I look out at their faces. It is my first day of kindergarten, not quite three months after the accident. I don't understand why this is necessary, but I will come to love Miss Black for thinking to do this.

Earlier that morning Mom and I had walked the several blocks from my house to Nelson Elementary School. There were a lot of kids on the playground when we arrived, and I wanted to play, but I stood close to Mom, watching. Miss Black and the other kindergarten teacher came out and lined us up at the classroom door before we were allowed to enter.

The classroom seemed a magical place, with tables of paints and clay, and a playhouse area with pint-sized kitchen appliances, including a stove and sink and cupboards. I especially liked snack time, which usually featured graham crackers covered with chocolate frosting.

I remember especially loving story time, when Miss Black would sit on a tiny chair in front of a large round rug, and all of us would sit cross-legged while she read to us. A time when I could escape into the lull and world of stories, words that drifted over us, weaving a web of protection and comfort that I escape to whenever possible still today.

Automobile factories and wood pulping mills fueled the economy of my hometown—and all of Western Michigan in the mid-twentieth century. When the wind blew from the north, the stench from the paper mill on the southern edge of Muskegon Lake wafted over downtown. My mom's best friend, Norma, lived with her family in the suburb of North Muskegon on the north side of the lake. Muskegon Heights, which was primarily African-American, was just east and south of downtown. Two of the three Meier Cleaners plants my dad operated were in Muskegon Heights, and when I was old enough to work for him, it was there I learned about prejudice and—from my dad—tolerance. On the southwest, as the city population expanded, the suburb of Norton Shores grew. My parents would build a house there when I was in junior high.

Routine, it's said, breeds boredom, but it also establishes place and time and provides a stability that can be comforting when all else around you is in turmoil. We walked to St. Joe's for Mass every Sunday. My dad went to work early every morning. Supper was always on the table at six, just after Dad walked through the door. We sat down together, and Dad said the blessing: *In the name of the Father, and the Son, and the Holy Ghost...Bless us, O Lord, and these, Thy gifts, which we are about to receive...*

We ate the same meal every night: meat, potatoes and canned vegetables. Sometimes we would have a Jell-O salad with celery or mandarin oranges. After dinner, we had dessert, usually homemade pie or cake with ice cream. If there was no pie or cake, we made do with cookies. My father loved dessert. Even years later, when it was only my mom and dad at home, they still shared dessert every night—a comforting routine, one of the many daily constructs we create to ignore the passage of time.

In Michigan, the seasons are distinct, glaringly so.

Winter was punishing icy blasts of wind and snow. Drifts grew and withered with each passing storm, moving from one side of the road to the other, or building to piles at the beaches and parks.

Spring was walking to church on Easter morning wearing a pale yellow or pink Easter dress and matching straw hat, my gloved hand thrust between my dad's strong, boxy fingers. Tulips and daffodils greeted us from the neighbors' gardens as we walked to church.

Summer was swimming in Lake Michigan with my dad and siblings at dusk, the lake water still warm from the day, then running up the stairs to have s'mores by the fireside as mosquitoes buzzed our ears.

Fall...well, fall is my favorite time of year. The leaves changing color on the maples, oaks and elms; the acrid smell of leaf piles smoldering in the street after a day of raking. The sweet bite of the apples we bought from the vendor who drove the streets hawking fruit from the back of his truck.

The milkman placed fresh bottles of milk at the front door every two or three days. And the egg man—a local farmer— brought fresh eggs to the house every week. There was a farmer's market on the outskirts of town every Saturday where we bought cherries, blueberries and raspberries, tomatoes, peaches and plums in summer, apples and pears in fall, and in winter, butternut and acorn squashes. In the summer months, my mother would often buy a bushel of one fruit or another and then spend the next several days canning.

All of these things happened predictably—year after year—creating a sense of serenity and comfort in the certainty of sameness.

And every few months I went into the hospital for more surgery.

Hughes Procedure

Nov. 29, 1961 — Surgeon's notes: Reconstruction of left upper eyelid by Hughes procedure, release of ectropion of the lower eyelid, repair of the resulting defect by covering with full-thickness skin graft from upper chest.

Mom carries my small red suitcase into my room. Surgery is scheduled for the next morning. After a nurse helps me into a hospital gown, she boosts me into a tall steel-sided crib. Hospital rules require children under seven to be in cribs, for safety. I hate them; I haven't been in a crib since I was an infant.

In the morning, they come with shots to relax and calm me. No food, no water. I become woozy, my body covered with a thin, scratchy blanket.

Mom arrives. And then they come for me, the masked ones from the OR, with green scrubs and caps on their heads. I have to scoot from the crib, moving my bottom and then my upper body over to the cold, flat gurney.

Mom holds my hand as we roll down the hallways and into the elevators, then down more fluorescent white hallways to the operating room. When we reach the big double doors beyond which she cannot come, I hear her say, "I'll be here when you get back. Love you." And she lets me go.

The surgical nurses who attended me over the years for the most part have become a blur, but there was one, I'll call her Anne, who embodied an angelic presence in the OR.

Her head is bathed in light from behind, so she seems to glow in her mask and green cap. She holds my hand and pats me soothingly, saying, "It's okay. Don't cry; it's going to be all right."

Dr. Kislov arrives and I see he is smiling behind his mask. I am very good at reading his face behind the cloth. I know when he is scowling, or perplexed, or exasperated if something isn't working the way he wants it to. I can sense his pursed lips when his eyebrows knit together, and know he is concentrating on a particular problem. His hair is caught up in a boxy green cap tied at the back, and his horn-rimmed glasses reflect my small, frightened face back to me. When he smiles, it stretches the mask and I feel as if I have done something extraordinary, something worthwhile. It makes me happy, even in my terror.

After a few minutes he nods to the anesthesiologist and gives me a pat on the arm. "Okay, Marcia," he says in his thick German accent, "we'll see you shortly, eh?"

I awake and throw up. I can smell the sickly-sweet aroma of the ether. My eyes are bandaged and I don't know where I am. My hands are tethered to the bedside bars. A nurse comes in and murmurs some reassuring words, words meant to calm me, but they only make me more anxious.

Where am I? Why can't I see?
Where is my mom?

Ten days after surgery, Mom and I went downtown to Dr. Kislov's office to have my stitches out. The office was in a two-story modern-looking building and there was a soda fountain on the first floor. Mom promised to buy me a malted milkshake after the stitches were out.

Dr. Kislov's office was paneled in dark wood, with boxy couches covered in green fabric.

"Hello, Marcia," Dr. Kislov said. "How are you today, eh?"

He brought his face close to mine, staring at the wounds, gently probing with his fingers, assessing the dozens of stitches he had sewed into it. I could smell his aftershave and the antiseptic on his fingers.

"Okay, up on the table."

As I lay on the examining table, he leaned over and again peered closely at my face, his thick dark brows furrowed. Mom held my arms across my chest then, and he began to tug at each suture with a long tweezer, stretching the thread so he could snip it with a scissors. He gently tugged the suture from my tender skin. I started to cry, and Dr. Kislov said, "If you cry, I will send your mother out of the room, ja?"

NO! I thought. *No.* So I sucked in my breath and blinked back my tears.

Carl Jung wrote that we all carry various archetypes within our psyches. Primary among them are The Self (sometimes called The Divine Child), The Shadow (where we hold repressed feelings, desires, instincts, and shortcomings), The Anima (the feminine side of the male psyche) or Aminus (the male side of the female psyche), and The Persona (the person we present to the world). But there are literally hundreds of other archetypes. Mine include the artist, the teacher, the storyteller, and the hermit. More than any other, though, I have been guided (or driven) by the Wounded Child, my deepest self.

Integrating one's archetypes—all those selves—means being able to understand and blend them so that, ultimately, we become whole beings. I have come to see that I had compartmentalized and stuffed away my Wounded Child, just as I had compartmentalized and stuffed away questions about my relationship with my mother. The more I explored, the more I saw that my Wounded Child had subconsciously dictated my responses to almost everything in my life. Throughout my childhood, my primary concern was survival, and the tools I developed to survive were independence, mistrust, strength, and a fierce determination someday to say "NO."

I was young once
scarred and circling
and full of premonition
I would have bitten him if I could
champed down on his fingers
as he traced the ridges on my face
bitten clean through to bone, just
to make sure he got the message,
made my hands rigid
pushed him away and screwed up
my mouth and said NO
very loudly
until maybe the air in the room
would disappear
and he would disappear
and I would bob up in another place,
and my mom would smile at me and say,
there, there.

DIVISION

Jan. 11, 1962 — Surgeon's notes: Division of tarsorrhaphy of left eyelids.

KINDERGARTEN WAS A SAFE PLACE, a place where it seemed I was accepted unconditionally. No one asked about my face or teased me.

That would change in the fall when I started first grade at St. Joe's.

My sister and I walked the three blocks to school each morning, past modest brick and clapboard houses. Street trees shaded the sidewalk where we walked. Generally there were no fences between houses.

St. Joe's was the German parish. Within a mile or two in differing directions were St. Michael's, the Polish parish, St. Jean's, the French parish, and St. Mary's, the Irish parish.

My dad and all his siblings attended St. Joseph's School, just as my siblings and I did. Faith was important to my grandparents, and my parents. In fact, my dad's oldest brother, David, joined the seminary after high school and served as a Jesuit priest the rest of his life. Helen, the second-oldest, followed her brother's example and entered the convent at eighteen, becoming a Dominican nun. Later we often joked that having two of their children in religious orders guaranteed Heaven for my grandparents.

My dad used to love to tell a story about one Sunday dinner when he was a boy. The parish priest had been invited. With six brothers and sisters, one learned quickly to grab the food as soon as grace was said. Otherwise you might not get any. So on this Sunday night, as soon as the "amen" was uttered, Dad's hand shot out for the chicken. My grandmother kicked him, hard, under the table. Then she smiled at the priest and passed him the chicken.

From my first day at St. Joe's, I struggled. The other children taunted and shunned me on the playground. It was black asphalt surrounded by chain-link fence, and stretched the length of the school behind and wrapped around the side toward the rectory, where Father lived. There was an old-fashioned swing set and slide, and markings on the asphalt for Four Square. Long jump ropes and balls would come out at recess. I would linger on the sidelines whenever there was a game, hoping someone might invite me to join in.

"Tell the scar-face to find someone else to play with..." they'd say, or they would ignore me until I slinked away. When they were choosing sides for dodge ball, I came to know I would be the last chosen. I learned to expect not to be included, and spent most of my recesses alone. I made up imaginary playmates who didn't care what I looked like. One day in the lunchroom a kid said I had train tracks on my face.

My response was to act out, mouth off to the kids, the nuns. I don't really remember misbehaving, but I have vivid memories of having chalk and erasers thrown at me by the nuns, or having other kids laughing and pointing at me, or being ordered to the cloakroom as punishment.

It is dark. I am sitting on the damp floor among the galoshes and rubbers. Coats and jackets hang on iron hooks overhead. I have done something bad, perhaps talked back to Sister. Again. It is a familiar place, a place that is both eerily quiet and roaring with recriminations. Through the closed door, I can hear Sister speaking to the kids in the classroom. Her voice is light-hearted and the kids respond enthusiastically. I sit in the dark, breathing in the wet wool.

Several months after the accident, Mom and Dad took me to court. A suit had been filed to determine who would pay what were expected to be long-term hospital bills. Mr. Benn, the man who hit me, and his wife were there. He was sitting up in a box by the judge.

"Mr. Benn, how old are you?" an insurance company attorney asked.

"Sixty-seven."

"And how long have you been driving?"

"Fifty-two years."

"And do you remember what happened on the morning of June 17th, at the corner of Fourth and Mason streets?"

"Yes, of course."

"Would you tell the court what you remember?"

"I stopped at the stop sign and when it was clear I drove through the intersection."

"Did you see this young girl walking her bike across the street?"

"No, I didn't."

"Why?"

"I am blind in my left eye. I didn't know she was in the intersection." He started to weep. "I didn't see her...."

The judge invited me to go up and sit in the witness box. He kindly asked me my name, how old I was and what grade I was in. As I answered, I realized he was looking at my face, trying to determine for himself the extent of the damage done. What he saw was a raw and ragged cheek, a missing upper eyelid and gaping hole where the lower lid used to be. That thick stringy connection holding the lids together. My lower lip split and the scar on my chin jutting down toward my neck. He saw my smile, just for him, through the scars.

After the hearing, Mr. Benn approached my parents in the courthouse hallway.

"Words can't express how sorry I am," he said. Muriel, standing next to him, fought back tears.

"May I bring her a gift, a baby doll?" He looked down at me. "I would be so happy if you would call me Grandpa Benn."

They did not tell him no. They told me to take the doll and call him Grandpa Benn.

Wherever you are now, Mr. Benn, here's what I want you to know: You are not my grandpa. You will never be my grandpa. And I will never call you Grandpa Benn again. Do you hear me?

You are not forgiven.

What made you think you could go around driving blind in your left eye? How in anyone's world did that seem like a good idea? You could have maimed more children, or killed them.

I wish they had thrown you in jail.

You feel bad? How about what I feel?

You feel guilty? Remorseful?

Am I supposed to feel sorry for you?

You went to my parents with baby dolls and all your guilt and asked them if I would please call you Grandpa Benn.

How dared you!

How dared *they* say yes?

Mr. Benn, maybe you were a nice man, with a wife and kids and grandkids. A home, I imagine, small tables decorated with your wife's crocheted lace and colorful afghans thrown over the davenport arms. Cozy pillows stitched with quaint sayings. A teapot on the stove. I imagine you had all that, and still you got behind the wheel of a car when you couldn't see out of your left eye, and drove down the street.

Damn you to hell, Mr. Benn.

MICHAEL

"WHY DO YOU THINK the accident happened?"

Michael and I are sitting in his airy office. It is early 2006 and I've been coming to therapy for about two months. Something reminds me of sitting in Dr. Kislov's office, waiting to see him, all those years ago. Perhaps it is the serenity of the setting, the nuanced invitation to consider my face, even though that is the last thing I want to do.

"What do you mean?" I ask.

"Whose fault was it?"

"Obviously, the guy who hit me," I say.

He smiled. "Yes, that's true. But why did he hit you?"

"He was blind in his left eye. He didn't see me."

"Uh-huh. But why didn't he see you?"

"I don't know…. Maybe it was meant to happen," I say.

"Why?"

I shrug. "Maybe I was meant to be hurt for another purpose. I've always felt like I survived for a reason. Now I'm not so sure."

I picked at the threads of a soft white throw pillow next to me on the couch. Looked out the window at the jacarandas, their purple blossoms long gone.

"Do you believe in fate?" Michael asked.

"I don't know. I don't think things happen because God wills it, like it's pre-ordained."

"Do you think you could have prevented it?"

I pause. My mom's words drift back to me.

"If I hadn't walked into the crosswalk…"

"You think you could have stopped the car?"

"I should have seen it."

"Say you had. How quickly do you think you could have gotten out of the way? You were in the middle of the crosswalk."

It was as if I was there again. The car is stopped at the intersection, and now it is coming at me.

I couldn't have gotten out of the way. No one could have.

It was not my fault.

It was not my fault!

A huge burden lifting.

"But why me?"

"Do you believe in God?" Michael asked me.

I had to think about this. The God of my childhood was patriarchal, judgmental, distant. Like my mother. I've never been able to relate to that God. But I feel connected to my Catholic childhood. Maybe connected isn't the right word. Perhaps I clung to the only faith experience I had, even though it was and remains a painful place for me.

"When I got married, it was in the church."

"Why was that so important to you?" Michael asked.

"Honestly, I didn't know at the time. I remember feeling that I wanted to be married in the church I grew up with, even though I no longer believed in the institution. I know that sounds crazy. My dad wasn't very happy with me. But I loved my uncle, Father Dave, who married us. I wanted someone I cared about to officiate. But I also knew it was a sham."

"So, where does God come in? What do you believe?"

"I don't know what I believe anymore."

"No, I think you do," Michael said. "I think you have some very well-formed beliefs about faith. What do you believe?"

What did I believe? I was so confused and felt adrift spiritually. I have always felt a connection somehow with "God," but it is not the God most people think of when they think about Christianity. I have always felt a strong longing, an awareness of something universal and powerful, unreachable, untouchable. A presence I sometimes feel in my body, in my chest and throat.

"Did God cause your accident?" Michael asked.

"I don't believe God—or whatever higher power or essence—makes bad things happen."

"If God didn't cause your accident, and you weren't to blame, why did it happen?"

"I don't know. I guess it just happened...I guess it just happened."

I thought about that. If no one causes things to happen, then no one is to blame, and also no one has control. Not God. Not me.

"There's almost a sense of, I don't know, freedom in that," I said.

"It's called existential freedom. Realizing that everything that happens is not connected in any way to what you or anyone else can or might do. That understanding provides the freedom to live without worry or fear."

It was a watershed moment, one I would return to over and over as I tried to place the events of my life in perspective.

I had blamed myself for the accident all these years.

My mother's words to me when I awoke in the hospital had fallen on fertile soil: *"We told you never to cross the street without looking."*

She'd blamed me.

And all the pain, the punishments, the surgeries, and St. Joseph's school, people staring—I believed I deserved it.

Eyelashes

April 6, 1962 — Surgeon's notes: Composite graft from left eyebrow into the left upper eyelid, transplanting hair of the eyebrow as lashes of upper eyelid.

I AWAKE. I am blind. My head is bandaged. I am anxious and afraid; no one is here. Then I am floating near the ceiling. I look down and see my body, head wrapped in gauze and tape, lying in the hospital bed. Intravenous tubing runs from a pole next to the bed into my arm. I watch the liquid drip into my veins. I hear the hiss of the oxygen tank next to the bed. I see the bed table nearby. I see the waist-high counter along the wall, with trays and medical instruments atop it. I float there for what seems a long time, watching, absorbing the scene, trying to comprehend how I can be in the bed and at the ceiling at the same time.

A nurse walks in and I am back in my body, lying on the bed, as she explains she has come to check the dressings on my face.

At midlife, I was struck by the realization that whenever I thought of myself, I did not see my face. There was only an essence, like that disembodied self floating at the ceiling, a bright being without shape or form. Body-less. As if, because

65

I had to give over my body to nurses and doctors and hospitals as a child—a body that I believed, at my deepest level, was disfigured and useless— it was safer and more accurate to see myself as essence, just personality.

In time, I began to see my faces—separate and many. There is the young ravaged face that others saw; the unmolested five-year-old face that exists only in a black-and-white photo that hangs on my wall; the face people tell me today they see as beautiful, though I still don't believe them. My long limbs became visible to me; my thin awkward frame with its patchwork of skin grafts on my stomach, chest, legs, transformed into a physical house I could inhabit. But still, the essence face is the only one that allows me to move through the world.

When I was young, people often asked about my face. Especially kids, who were often unkind or unthinking. As I grew older, I developed a standard response. Adults seem to know better than to ask, "What happened to your face?" And in fact, over time I rarely thought of my face and how I looked to others. I can't remember a friend or even a new acquaintance in recent years who has asked about my face. Eventually, somehow the question comes up and I explain. And usually the friend will say, "I don't even notice it."

But when I was in my late thirties, I was invited to read to a class of second-graders at an elementary school in Santa Barbara. I was about halfway through the picture book when a kid sitting in the front raised his hand.

"Yes?" I said.

"You look like a witch!" he said.

My stomach clenched.

"Your eye, it looks like a witch."

The other kids laughed. In a flash I was at St. Joe's again. I felt like crawling under the chair. But instead I smiled and explained what had happened to me, adding a lesson about always looking both ways before crossing a street. I read the rest of the book and escaped as fast as I could. I hadn't felt that stab of pain and shame in a long time.

A week later, I got a packet in the mail. It contained letters of apology from the whole class, including a note from the teacher saying how embarrassed and sorry she was for the rudeness of the boy. I threw them all in the trash.

I asked earlier, how is the self created? Certainly the physical is a major part of how we become who we are. Our sense of self is closely tied to the image we see, or imagine we see, in a mirror. The face is the first thing people look at. How people respond to our faces is internalized from our earliest childhood.

Since my face had been rejected by almost everyone I encountered from the time I was five, I believed my face—and my scarred body—were worthless. I began to live in my head, without consciousness of my body. I slouched; I hid behind oversized clothing. In high school I let my long hair fall to hide my face. I moved into that essence person whom my family loved, if no one else seemed to. I did not have a single friend until fourth grade, when a little girl named Debbie Deyman moved to Muskegon from Tennessee and started school at St. Joe's. Debbie was new, and I was scarred. We became fast friends. I loved her mom, who had a lilting Tennessee accent, and throughout that year and next we often slept over at each other's houses, and clung to each other during school. My scars didn't seem to matter to Debbie, and she gave me the hope that maybe I could have other friends. Gradually over the years I made my way out of my shell.

Away from St. Joe's, I found acceptance among new friends in junior high and high school, and college gave me the opportunity to be the person I desperately wanted to be. It was safe, finally, to reveal myself to others, to explore new interests and forge a path toward a career in journalism, where, ironically, I found safety in interviewing and writing about others, turning attention away from myself, even while getting the immense satisfaction of seeing my name in small type at the top of a news story.

Even with this newfound confidence, it wasn't until I was in my fifties that I began to learn to drop out of my head into my body. To re-embody myself, to feel comfortable in my physical being. My default even today is to stay in my head, to intellectualize everything, and to keep emotional feelings and physical sensations at bay. I paid a terrible price for those years of rejecting my physical self, and it has been a long journey to be able to feel physical pleasure from touch, mine or someone else's, and to be sensual in all senses of the word.

"I think my marriage is falling apart."

It's January 2006, and I am sitting on Michael's white couch for the first time.

"What makes you believe that?" he asks.

Where to begin?

My husband and I were good friends. But I hadn't felt an emotional or physical connection with him for a long time. I knew there were reasons that had to do with his own upbringing and family dysfunction. And I would come to understand that my own emotional deficiencies contributed to this. But I never imagined our relationship would wither to a shell of sadness, anger and recrimination.

I'm not fond of the phrase "mid-life crisis." It might rather be described as a mid-life reckoning, an assessment of days lived; for me, it was a growing sense that I was not doing what I was on the planet to do. I was shocked to feel that my life was half over and I had accomplished little—that, even more, I had ignored my purpose for being.

Jung theorized that this questioning at midlife is actually a key to individuation, or the process of integrating all the various aspects of personality into a cohesive whole. This is sometimes called self-actualization or self-awareness. For me, it hit with a suddenness and intensity for which I was unprepared. And it started with my fiftieth birthday.

Christmas Eve is a terrible time to have a birthday. You share with half the world a day that is supposed to celebrate *you*. And more often than not, people forget.

But as my fiftieth drew near, I couldn't help dreaming of all kinds of wonderful things my husband might do to show he cared. I had thrown a huge surprise party for his fiftieth. Surely he would want to express love for me?

I tried to be realistic, since usually I got a card and whatever I carefully wrote on a wish list. But still, I kept thinking, fifty is a big birthday. And our daughter by then was thirteen, old enough to offer some guidance to her dad.

On that morning, I woke to birthday wishes from the whole family, and Kendall urged me to open her gifts: a piece of flagstone hand-painted in a Southwestern design—she knew that New Mexico is one of my favorite places—and a beaded bracelet. They were perfect.

Then I opened John's gifts: a set of four nondescript coasters to protect furniture from drink marks. And a mini-tool set.

I didn't know what to say. I thought, *We've been married twenty-four years and this is all you could think of?* I would have been happier with a gift card from Borders Books. At least that would have shown he knew I liked books. Did he know me at all? Did he care enough to know me?

I got through the day, but later that evening I went into my bedroom and sat on my bed and cried. I thought, *My marriage is over.* When Kendall knocked gently on the door and came in and sat beside me, she didn't ask why I was crying. She knew. "I'm sorry you're so disappointed, Mom," she said.

A couple of days later I asked John to go for a walk. We took our two Australian shepherds and went out to Ellwood, a long beautiful stretch of parkland and bluffs that runs for several miles along the ocean north of Santa Barbara. We strolled in silence for a long time as the dogs romped ahead of us. I knew he would never open a conversation about our relationship, so eventually I did.

"John, I don't know what's happened to us over these past few years, but I want more than this."

He was silent. We kept walking.

"I need emotional engagement. I need intimacy."

He nodded.

I asked him about the birthday presents. Didn't he know of anything I would like to have? Something that was personal? Something that reflected my likes and interests?

He was silent.

And then I said something I had never said to him, even when things were really bad between us.

"If you can't give me what I need, I'll leave you."

It may have sounded like a threat, but it wasn't. At that point, I was simply stating a fact.

Robert Grudin, in his lovely book, *Time and the Art of Living*, writes: "We lose what is valuable in [relationships]—love, joy, communality—less through conflict and tragedy than through long series of shadowy and often unconscious refusals. Withdrawing, forgetting, falling out of touch, ignoring or avoiding or withholding the unpretentious but essential details of friendship, destroy more relationships than death or anger and tend to isolate their perpetrators quite early in the solitary confinement of old age. To the Latin adage *Qui tacet consentit* ('He who is silent consents'), we might add another, *Qui non agit negat* ('He who does not act, denies')."

We were both complicit in the former and the latter.

As I look back at that time, I realize my sense of abandonment reverberated through all my relationships, not just with my husband. Certainly with my mother, who had been distant most of my life. I was close to my sister Cherie, but she had moved to Oregon with her husband in 1996. I knew she didn't intentionally leave *me*; they were making a choice as a couple to start a new life somewhere that would be better for them. Still, it had felt like abandonment.

My dad had died four years before—the one person I always knew would take care of my heart, would be there whenever I needed him. And while I knew intellectually, of course, that he, too, didn't "leave" me, his death compounded my sense of abandonment by those I loved. It may in fact have been the triggering event.

I suppose I could also say that, in a way, I felt abandoned by Dr. Kislov. We had moved to California when I was eighteen, and I never saw him again. Just as I stuffed all my feelings about my childhood and my surgeries down to a deep place, I buried Dr. Kislov. I didn't understand the relationship I had with him, nor had I ever considered how I felt about the person in my childhood who—perhaps more than any other—had held the power to determine the shape and direction of my life.

ROTATION

May 25, 1962 — Surgeon's notes: Excision of entire scar and split-thickness skin graft of the left cheek. Rotation of a large local pedicle flap from lower portion of the left cheek and upper portion of the left neck.

YOU ARE LYING IN YOUR CRIB, head bandaged, when you hear Dr. Kislov's voice. He has come in with a nurse.

"We are going to change the dressing now, Marcia, and I will allow you to see from your right eye. But you must promise to be quiet. Ja? If you aren't, we will put the bandage back on? Ja? Understand?"

You nod.

He begins to cut the tape near your right ear, carefully and slowly peeling it back. The nurse holds her hands over yours as he snips the gauze around your head. Cool air on your skin. The smell of adhesive mixed with dried blood. You feel him lift the patch from your right eye and you sense the brightness of the room. Slowly you open your eye. Dr. Kislov's face leans close and he smiles. His face is so familiar, as familiar as your dad's. Even today you can see his eyes through his horn-rimmed glasses, his broad cheeks, his clean-shaven face, his strong jutting chin, the gap between his front teeth.

"There!" he says. "Now, remember, you must remain quiet."

And you are, for a time. But a few days later, you are in your crib, happy and bouncing up and down while holding onto the side rail. At that moment, Dr. Kislov walks past your room. He looks in and immediately you see his scowl, his anger. You are instantly remorseful. He shakes his finger at you. You drop down and lie quietly. A few minutes later he comes in with a nurse. For a moment, you see your face reflected in his eyeglasses. His mouth is set in a tight line. He doesn't say a word, just re-bandages your head with patches over both eyes. You are blind once again.

St. Joe's was a daily nightmare. The cruelty and rejection of the nuns and children, the feeling of humiliation and shame and pain. Finally one morning—I was probably eight or nine—I started off from home in my green plaid uniform, but halfway to St. Joe's, I stole down the alley and hid between the houses. I waited a long time. Maybe if it was too late for school, Mom would let me stay.

It was mid-morning when I started back toward home. I don't know what magic I really wanted. That she would understand how terrible school was? That she would comfort me? But as soon as she saw me standing on the front porch, she was angry.

"What are you doing here?" she demanded. "Why aren't you in school?"

I stammered. She grabbed me by the arm and dragged me back to St. Joe's. I cried most of the way.

My mother didn't have patience for weakness. She was strong. Later in life I came to realize that strength can also be warm, can give, can love. When I look back, I see how strong she had to be. Lost two babies, raised four others, dealt with tragedy after tragedy. And her way of being strong was to drag a weeping child back to school.

What was she feeling when she saw me creep back home? Exasperation? Worry that I would miss lessons? Fear that I was being coddled if she let me stay home? What lessons had she learned growing up that made her punish me for not going to school?

When we arrived, she marched me into the classroom and physically threw me at Sister, who took me by the scruff of the neck and pushed me down into my desk. I could hear the other kids laughing and snickering, and I was overwhelmed with humiliation. I did not see my mother leave.

Several more times I hid in the alley, crouching down in the bushes, waiting a little longer each time, believing if it was late enough in the morning she'd relent and let me stay home. But each time she hauled me back to school, and when she started to spank me with her paddle, I gave up.

For most of my childhood, I experienced painful things, both emotionally and physically. But everyone told me that not only was it for my own good, it wasn't really traumatic, it didn't really hurt the way I knew it did, that people didn't really mistreat me, or that whatever happened to me was a direct result of my own misbehavior. I *deserved* it.

"We told you never to cross the street without looking..."

This was the lie of my childhood, and it led to beliefs and behaviors as an adult that almost destroyed my ability to live as a whole person.

Forced to deny my own experience and accept what others insisted was true, I splintered.

I was thirty-five when we decided to adopt a child. I didn't want children before then, while I was preoccupied with building my journalism career. My sister Molly had two children, and in my thirties I began to feel a deep longing for a child—a child we could love and nurture and watch grow. For several years we tried to have a biological child, but we couldn't.

So we signed up with a non-profit adoption agency and began to learn about open adoption, which was becoming more widespread. We had to create a resume of sorts, which we sent to all our family and friends announcing we were looking for birthparents, and which was also used by the adoption center with birthparents interested in relinquishing their child.

Here is the letter we wrote in September 1991:

Dear birthmother,

We can hardly imagine the feelings you must have at this moment. But we know this: You're looking for a couple to raise your child, and give him or her a home where honesty, integrity and love rule, where values are translated into actions. We want to offer that to you and your child.

We have been married nine years, and have lived in Santa Barbara since 1985, when we moved here to be closer to Marcia's family. Most Sundays are reserved for dinner at Grandma's (Marcia's mom and dad's)! Marcia is a newspaper editor and writer. She plans to take several months' leave to spend with the baby when he or she arrives, and will have at-home care when she goes back to work. John is an architectural and construction project manager. We've known professional success. For some years we have wanted to also know the enrichment and responsibilities of parenthood. Yet we have been unable to conceive.

We enjoy spending time with friends and family, and are anxious to share and nurture a baby in the environment of caring that we have come to know among our closest loved ones.

Marcia is a great lover of animals, and has been a volunteer at the Santa Barbara Zoo (we have two kitties and only a lack of acreage keeps us from having a menagerie). She is looking forward to sharing her appreciation of nature and wildlife with a toddler.

John is anticipating the excitement of being a new father, and looks forward to sharing with a child his enthusiasm for sports (especially football!), and for gourmet cooking. Our friends have said they can just see John walking around the kitchen checking the sauces with a baby on his hip.

We can offer your child a loving, stable home with an involved extended family. We believe in strong family bonds and a nurturing and loving environment for children.

If you would like to discuss the possibility of us adopting your child, please call us collect, or call our adoption counselor, Dani Steiger, at The Adoption Center in Santa Barbara.

We knew we wanted an infant, but other questions forced a lot of soul-searching. We had to think about not only our own prejudices and preferences, but what would be best for the child, as well. Could we adopt a child of another race? Yes. A child with medical problems? I struggled with the idea, knowing what my parents had gone through. Ultimately we marked the boxes: white infant.

Nine months later, we got a call from The Adoption Center. A young woman in Iowa had chosen us from a stack of resumes. She was only two weeks from her due date. She and the birthfather were not married and had a son not quite a year old. Things were rocky between them, to the point that he had sabotaged potential agreements with three other couples before us. We agreed to talk with her on the phone. I have little recollection of the things we talked about. I think we may have asked a lot of questions about her and her family, and her decision to relinquish. The birthfather was with her, so we spoke with him as well. He and my husband seemed to connect, and by the end of the call he promised to support the adoption. They were both eighteen years old.

Less than a week after that first conversation, we got a call from The Adoption Center. She was in labor. Could we fly to Iowa for the birth? It was a Friday morning, and we scrambled. We made arrangements to take a red-eye flight out of Los Angeles at midnight. We still had one more approval appointment with the state, and arranged to stop at their Los Angeles offices that afternoon.

When we arrived the next morning, we drove from Des Moines to her little hometown on the Mississippi River. We knocked on her apartment door. She opened it, big as a house, her son clinging to her legs. She smiled, a beautiful smile framed by her long dark hair.

"It was false labor," she said. "So they sent me home."

She invited us in and we talked for a long time. She didn't know the sex of the child—hadn't wanted to know—but suspected it was another boy. She asked, Did we have names picked out? And we told her our choices. "Those are nice," she said. Later she confided that she had hoped we'd let her have a say in the name, but she liked the ones we had picked.

For the next six days we stayed in her hometown, met her mother and sisters and their children, drove to the river, had meals with the family. She and the birthfather had a fight just before we arrived and he had disappeared. We fretted. Would he come back in time for the birth? Should we stay until the baby is born or fly home? We stayed. She finally went into real labor a week after we arrived. She asked us to drive her to Iowa City; she would give birth at the University of Iowa Hospitals there. Just before we left, she got a phone call from the birthfather. He was in Cincinnati. We offered to fly him to Iowa City that evening. On our way out of town we stopped to drop her son off with her sister. But first we drove through the local McDonald's, where she bought her one-year-old a cheeseburger and fries.

Iowa City was an hour and a half away, and we counted the minutes between contractions all the way. When we arrived it was mid-afternoon, and by the time she got settled into a room the labor had slowed. The birthfather arrived about 11:30 p.m. He was tall and thin, with longish blond hair, and our meeting was awkward but cordial. He went into the birthing room with her for the rest of the night. We lounged around the waiting rooms, walked the hallways, tried to sleep fitfully in waiting room chairs. We kept checking in throughout the night, waiting, waiting. At 7:47 a.m., Kendall arrived. The nurses had come to get us, and we stood outside the birthing room door. When it opened, it was the birthfather who carried Kendall out to us, pink and tiny, wrinkled and serene. He offered her to us. We cut the remaining stump of her umbilical cord, with a little help from the nurse, and we took her into the nursery, where they did her newborn assessment. We helped give her a bath, and I have a picture of me in the rocking chair in the nursery giving her her first bottle.

What a magical time that was. The birthmother and Kendall stayed at the hospital for two days. Whenever the nurses would ask one of us if they could do some test or other, the birthmother and I would both say, "Ask her mother(birthmother)." When Kendall was released, the nurses made two sets of footprints on certificates, for us and the birthparents.

We decided to go to a restaurant to say goodbye. Her mom and sisters were with us, and when we stood to leave, there were lots of tears and hugs and promises to stay in touch. And we have, though it has become more sporadic as the years have gone by.

We spent two more weeks in Iowa City with our newborn, waiting for the courts to approve our initial adoption. The hotel gave us a baby crib and a big rocking chair, and we washed out Kendall's baby clothes in the sink. As we waited, we ventured out to explore Iowa City when the rain stopped, and we watched the entire Democratic National Convention and most of the summer Olympics on TV. Finally we got the okay to come home, and we dashed to the Des Moines airport with our new baby and a brand-new car seat. Kendall slept through the entire flight, and when we arrived at LAX at midnight my mom and dad were there to greet us. We went to my aunt's house in Brentwood where we had an impromptu party with several of my cousins. When we finally got into our car to drive up to Santa Barbara it was 2 a.m. But we were home, and we were parents.

As she has grown, I have come to understand how deeply Kendall has been shaped by loss. Loss of her birthparents, loss of her dear grandfather, fear of losing her parents. Her sense of self is deeply affected by not only her own early childhood experiences, but by what happened before she was born. She will forever be an "adopted child," one whose birthparents, with whatever good intentions, chose to relinquish her. I know she struggles with this. Who would not? When she looks in the mirror, does she see her true self, or an "adopted child"? How will my daughter's early experiences of loss affect her ability to deal with the inevitability of more loss throughout her life? I wonder sometimes if my own self was shaped in part by the fact that I came along so quickly in the wake of my older brothers' deaths.

"I never had time to mourn them," my mother once said to me. Was I an interloper, then, an unwanted intrusion when all she wanted to do was grieve? In my deepest self, did I know this?

I have thought a lot about how the trauma I experienced affected me and those around me, and discovered there is a lot of research on the impacts of early trauma on children.

Children who experience multiple and/or chronic traumatic events—or complex trauma—often suffer serious social, emotional, neurological, physical, and sensory development problems. If the child's "attachment relationships," especially those with parents, are compromised, she will likely suffer a range of crippling issues. They include uncertainty about the reliability and predictability of the world, problems with boundaries, social isolation, difficulty with emotional self-regulation, chronic or pervasive depression, suicidal preoccupation, poor modulation of impulses, self-destructive behavior, substance abuse, problems focusing on and completing tasks, lack of a continuous and predictable sense of self, low self-esteem, feelings of shame and guilt, and disturbances of body image.

The only way to avoid these complications is to intervene early on with emotional and psychological support. "Psychological trauma in early childhood can have a tremendous negative impact as it can distort the infant, toddler or young child's social, emotional, neurological, physical and sensory development. This is especially true of young children who have experienced multiple and/or chronic, adverse interpersonal traumatic events through the child's care giving system" ("Complex Trauma in Early Childhood," American Academy of Experts in Traumatic Stress, online).

The U.S. Centers for Disease Control says this "'toxic stress' can lead to permanent changes in the development of the brain. The negative effects of toxic stress can be lessened with the support of caring adults. Appropriate support and intervention can help in returning the stress response system back to its normal baseline" ("The Effects of Childhood Stress on Health Across the Lifespan," CDC pamphlet, 2008).

Of course, there was no such help available when I was young. People didn't think to offer psychological or even emotional support to children who were hospitalized with traumatic injuries in the 1960s. Parents weren't allowed to stay overnight, siblings were not allowed to visit. Thankfully much has changed, and hospitals have realized how important parents and families are to healing. Most have drastically changed the way they treat young patients and their families. But no one that I know of ever suggested counseling for me or my family.

Mothers, more than any other family member, are the most critical to children being able to deal with physical and emotional trauma, threat or abuse. In his 1987 book, *Psychological Trauma*, Bessen A. ven der Kolk, M.D. discusses the strong mother-infant bond seen among both mammals and birds:

"Recent primate research confirms the view of Bowlby and Ainsworth that an attachment figure provides the infant with the security necessary to explore the limits of its surroundings, thus permitting exploration and affiliation even at some distance from the attachment figure.

"...Prospective studies on the long-term effects of loss of attachment bonds in humans are currently incomplete, but research by Spitz, Mahler and Cicchetti indicate that failure to develop such bonds is devastating. Small children, unable to anticipate the future, experience separation anxiety as soon as they lose sight of the mother. After the development of object constancy, overwhelming traumatic experiences cause a loss of trust that the separation call will be answered. In both children and adults, this may lead to temporary or lasting disruptions in the capacity to modulate emotions and engage in social affiliation. The clinical symptoms of this lost trust can be as severe as the symptoms of those in whom basic trust never developed."

In my case, I was protected by my father's deep love and care for me, which is what I attached to when my mother was unable to nurture me. But I developed a debilitating distrust of intimate relationships other than that with my dad. In addition, the message of my childhood was that other people rejected me because of how I looked. And this also led me to distrust the possibility of intimate relationships.

I struggled with the idea of ever having a boyfriend. Later, when John showed interest in me, I believed he was the only man who ever would, so I married him.

Today, after years of therapy, after a relationship with a man who loved me for who I am and being able to open up to him both emotionally and physically, I am at last capable of trust and joy in intimacy. But I know I'm not there completely.

Skin Graft

May 29, 1962 — Surgeon's notes: Split-thickness skin graft of remaining portion of the donor site of the pedicle flap.

I AM LYING in a hospital crib where they have tied me down, my right arm taped to a stiff board. There is a needle in my arm, and the tubing that runs to it delivers plasma, drop by tedious drop, into my veins. I watch the blood drip: one...two...three...four... from a fat bag on a pole. It takes a long time, but slowly the bag deflates until only the faint remnants of blood remain.

How long? An hour? Two? The nurse comes to free me, removes the needle, tapes a cotton ball to the inside of my arm. Bends my elbow and instructs me to keep it elevated for several minutes. Pats my leg, and leaves.

I was bitterly resentful of having to stay in a crib. Cribs were for babies. These cribs were large steel monstrosities with tall sides—cages, really. Because my hands were often tied to the sides, they became prisons. The crib, the cage, was another place indelibly linked with fear. Another part of my life in which I had no choice, no control.

If it was allowed, I would stand in the middle of the mattress holding onto the railings and look out the door and down the corridor. I knew the sounds of the nurses' footfalls. I could distinguish my mother's from the time she stepped out of the elevator. Knew how many steps she would take to round the corner into my room.

What I don't remember is whether she ever spoke to me. My memory of those times is of her silence. My mother sitting next to the crib, knitting. Sometimes she'd hold my hand through the bars. If we were allowed to lower the bars so she was close, that was when I felt safest.

Going to Catholic school meant attending Mass every weekday morning. We assembled in the classroom and trooped single-file over to the sanctuary. More than once I forgot my beanie or mantilla and with great exasperation Sister would pin a Kleenex on top of my head.

I had a hard time focusing on the Mass. I often grew faint after standing, sitting, and kneeling repeatedly. If I leaned back against the pew while kneeling, I would feel the sharp jab of Sister's knuckles into my back. During Lent we had to attend the Stations of the Cross every Friday afternoon, and the sickly sweet incense the priest waved up and down the aisles nauseated me.

I had a hard time paying attention. Looking back at what was going on in my life at the time, the continual surgeries, the pain and fear, it's hard to forgive the church's lack of compassion. Sister was always sighing over something I did. Once she threw a chalkboard eraser at me. Another time I was made to kneel on the hardwood floor in the corner. More often I was sent to sit in the dark cloakroom, alone among the familiar damp cloaks, galoshes and wet woolen mittens.

My mother and my husband were alike in many ways. Reserved, living in the shadow of a more outgoing partner. Despite all the trauma of my childhood, I was generally cheerful and optimistic, and later this aspect of my nature served me well and probably contributed to my success as a journalist.

With Mom, it wasn't that Dad was overbearing. It was that he was such an outsized personality, warm and gracious, generous of spirit and quick to laugh. He made people feel good about themselves, as he did with me. I could not have survived those early years without him. He was a comforting presence in a world that was often confusing and frightening.

My sister Cherie remembers our mother as a happy, outgoing person, someone who loved to go to parties and dance with my father. A woman of vibrancy and laughter. I knew she loved to dance, and I can remember her laughter, but as if from a distance. With me she never seemed happy. My memories of her are more muted, strafed by shades of gray, by the harshness of her paddle on my bottom, her sharp words, her long silences.

I was with my dad in 1999 when the doctor told him he had lung cancer. Stage III. Just a week later, the doctors said it was in his brain and bones: Stage IV. He started radiation and chemotherapy. They suggested a clinical trial, and our hopes were raised. Maybe he would get the experimental drug. Maybe it would stop the cancer. Months went by, and Dad got worse. By Thanksgiving, the doctors said there was nothing more they could do, and we gathered at the dinner table convinced he would not be with us at Christmas. We held a wake of sorts; a wake for the living. We stood to make speeches. There were a lot of tears and he seemed embarrassed by it, even a little irritated. As if we had already buried him.

But then, without the toxic drugs of chemotherapy, he started to feel better. Christmas was, if not joyful, an occasion of gratitude. Dad was still with us. In fact, he looked almost like his old self. Except he was so thin. And he gasped for breath.

One day, he was out walking. Not like he used to walk, miles down the bike path to the beach each day. But to the end of the street, which had become a chore. On the way back, he met our neighbor, Maggie, who had survived breast cancer.

"How are you, Bob?" she asked.

He stood there a moment, and then the tears slid down his handsome cheeks. She reached out, placed her hand on his arm, and squeezed.

After Christmas, I started driving Dad to his doctor appointments. I sat in the cancer center waiting room with him. We did a lot of waiting. A nurse would call out a name, and someone would stand and walk across the room. I wondered which of them would be here tomorrow, next month, next year. I knew that soon Dad wouldn't be, and I felt distraught, betrayed, grief-stricken. At forty-three, I was too young to lose my father.

As the weeks went by, Dad's face grew thinner, and he started to wince from the pain whenever anyone touched him. Still, he got up each day and dressed as if he were going to the office. At Easter, we gathered again as a family. It was clear it would be the last time.

We sat on the patio in the sun, and I have a photo of him from that day, smiling, with Kendall and me standing behind his lawn chair, leaning toward him. There is just a hint of sadness there, around his eyes and mouth. Two days later, I called the family doctor and said, "It's time for hospice." Then Mom and I told Dad the *doctor* thought it was time for hospice. It was a small subterfuge. He hadn't given up, but the rest of us had.

On the following Monday, the hospice nurse came to the house. Dad sat in his chair, dressed nicely; but for his gauntness, looking fit. As he filled out the forms, the nurse explained that one meant they would not try to resuscitate him. He stopped and looked at Mom. "What do you think, Pat?" he asked. After a moment, she said: "I wouldn't want them to keep *me* alive." Dad hesitated, just for a moment, and signed the form.

They moved a hospital bed into the extra bedroom, and set up an oxygen tank to help him breathe. It seemed odd, Dad sleeping in a room by himself. I wondered if Mom felt abandoned after sharing a bed with him for more than half a century. Once when I was little, I went into their bedroom early one morning. I had never noticed Dad holding Mom in bed, but the two of them were lying like spoons, and there was a smile on both of their faces.

On Wednesday, the hospice nurse came to check on Dad. When I stopped by later that afternoon, he was in his pajamas. He never got dressed again.

On Thursday, he fell in the bathroom. My brother had to help him up off the floor. His left arm and shoulder, riddled with bone cancer, were bruised and swelled monstrously. He went to bed. I did not see him that day.

On Friday afternoon, I went into the house and it was quiet. I walked down the hallway, and saw Dad sprawled crosswise on the bed, mouth agape. He looked a hundred years older than when I had seen him two days before. I rushed to find my brother, who was napping in the back bedroom. "Help!" I yelled. "Help me with Dad!"

He had fallen back across the bed, head bent against the hospital bed rail, legs outstretched, arms thrown wide from his body. It took all three of us, Mom, Chuck and me, to get him comfortably back into bed.

When the hospice nurse arrived, she started to place drops of morphine on his tongue, four and five at a time, and spoke loudly. "Bob, Bob, can you hear me?" He roused a little. We called my sisters, and Dad talked to them on the phone. But his eyes were closed. He was already engaged in the heavy business of dying.

So we sat and waited. Friends dropped by. Mom hovered like a ghost. Saying nothing. Wringing her hands. Hanging in the background. Or did it only seem that way?

Now I wonder if she felt she had been pushed to the sidelines. Because I took over, as I always do.

I sat sentry, holding his hand, dropping the pearls of morphine into his gaping mouth. I did not know if it helped, but I did it anyway. Late in the evening, Mom went to lie down. Did she resent my assertion? I assumed at the time she was simply exhausted.

I stayed with Dad, watched his chest rise and fall. Each pause between his breaths lengthened as the hour went by. Finally, he stopped breathing. I ran to get Mom. She fell across his chest and wept, making a whimpering sound almost like a puppy. Chuck came in and stood by the bedside, tears sliding down his cheeks.

Around midnight, the funeral home people came. The next day, Molly arrived and we went to make arrangements. We were sitting with the funeral director, remembering funny moments with Dad and laughing the way people do when they are grieving but don't yet realize it. When Mom chose a small mausoleum chamber for his urn, I asked about purchasing the one next to it. The man was kind and said he would hold it for two weeks for me and I could call back anytime. I never did.

Phillip Moffitt said, "One of the great challenges in life is to not allow the pretense of the difficult to shut down your heart."

Though I remember every moment, they flow together, so that now I distrust my own belief in the memory. Memory is porous, untrustworthy, and yet... I *know* in my being certain things, certain experiences come to me with not only vividness but unwavering conviction. When I write, I pull the memories from that deep space of knowing, of incontrovertible truth.

Did my mother love me? Yes. Was she devastated by and angry at my accident? Yes. Did she harbor jealous feelings about my relationship with my dad? Unquestionably. Did I love her? Without a doubt.

And yet, here I am a mature woman, wondering, questioning her treatment of me, her emotional abandonment, her lack of compassion when I tested her patience as a child, her inability or unwillingness to tell me she was proud of my accomplishments, proud of who I had become as an adult.

One of my mother's friends once told me she bragged about me during their bridge games. I was astonished. Why could she not say such things to me? It made me wonder whether my siblings had experienced something similar. Had she praised me when she was with them, just as she had always praised them around me?

So many questions. I realize I will never know the answers. My only option is this: forgiveness, both of her and of myself. And compassion. And letting go of regret for the things I did and didn't do.

Now my sister Molly is gone, too.

Am I right with their souls? I cannot tell.

There are two kinds of grief. There is the jarring and sharp kind. The initial pain, the deep-breath, Oh-my-God-no! kind of grief. When my boyfriend and I landed in Paris in February 2016, and I opened the text messages from my niece and sister saying Molly had suddenly died, this is the grief I felt. It was coupled with disorientation and disbelief. I needed to talk to them—what had happened? I asked them to recount the details over and over until it slowly sank in.

There is also a lingering grief, the kind that settles into long-term sadness, a sorrow and loss that remains in the heart. This is the grief I feel for my parents, and now, after time has passed, for Molly. This is the harder grief, I think. It re-emerges when you least expect it —on hearing a song, or catching the scent of your mother's favorite flower, or coming across a Facebook message your sister left two days before she died.

We had an uneasy relationship, Molly and I. I was hard on her. I didn't approve of her life choices (as if I had made any better ones), and I never let an opportunity go by to let her know. Two weeks after her death at age fifty-six, I found myself at a writing retreat, one I had planned for more than six months, and at which I hoped to work on this memoir. Instead, I ended up writing about Molly.

They said it was a withdrawal-induced seizure.

I remember how cute Molly was as a child. Bubbly and bright and so full of mischief.

I remember one day at Whiskeytown Lake when she was nineteen, how she stood on a big boulder above the waves, her long blonde hair accentuating her darling figure. I remember her beautiful smile that day.

I remember how much my mother loved her. How she'd light up when Molly walked into the room.

And I remember how Molly sank into pain medication addiction, and how much I blamed and judged her.

I remember how angry I was when she neglected her kids.

I remember that at five, my niece became the mom in the family, taking care of her younger brother—and Molly—all the years that followed.

I remember how angry I was when she divorced her children's father.

I remember that she adored horses and dogs and cats, that she loved with such a big heart.

I remember that she dreamed someday of owning a horse ranch, where she could ride and be with the creatures she loved.

I remember that for years we waited for her to arrive on Christmas—or Thanksgiving, or Easter—waited and waited, until we coined a phrase: We'll know she's here when we see the whites of her eyes.

I remember the tension of those holidays. Under the surface, the perpetual currents. And my anger at her for not being able to fulfill our holiday imaginings of a happy family.

I remember that her friends loved her—and also that she shared her drugs with them.

I remember mornings when she'd come to visit, and how in a drugged stupor she'd fall asleep at breakfast, her head lolling back and forth, almost pitching into her eggs and bacon.

I remember one day coming home and finding her passed out on the living room floor, the lamp knocked from the table.

I remember how she used to come to visit Mom, and together they would conspire to hide Mom's Vicodin.

I remember how her daughter tried over and over to get Molly to see how her life could be better.

I remember being embarrassed that she was my sister when she came to one of my book signings.

I remember that she never stopped talking. If we were on the phone, I listened, because as soon as I started to say something, she would talk over me.

I remember feeling resentful that she never asked about me.

I remember that Mom simply loved her—always. Forgave her—always. Believed in her—always.

I remember that when Mom died, Molly tried to be a part of the interment service, tried to help me with a reading I couldn't get through. And I rejected her help. I rejected her, again and again.

I remember that after Mom died, we rarely talked. I can't remember when I last saw her.

I remember that in recent years my resentment and judgments began to fade into compassion and love.

I remember that my attempts to reach out to her then were rebuffed. They were too late.

I remember how much I didn't give to her, and how much she needed.

I remember that she was absolutely convinced she'd win the Publisher's Clearinghouse Sweepstakes.

I remember the Facebook message she sent two days before she died. About how much she admired and loved me. I was surprised. I will always be grateful I responded, even clipped as it was. "Back at you, darlin'," I wrote.

LEAVING HOME

June 19, 1962 — Surgeon's notes: Division [again] of tarsorrhaphy of left upper and lower eyelids.

TEASING. Sadness. Constant hospitalizations. I decided to leave home. Packed a kerchief with peanut-butter-and-jelly sandwiches, added some cookies, and tied the whole parcel to a stick. Left a dramatic note—"I'm not worthy of living here!"— and struck out through downtown Muskegon, following the route I had seen us drive so many times. It was about three miles to my grandmother's house in Glenside, and McGrath Park was at the end of her street. I crossed the freeway at a stoplight near Nelson Elementary School, then walked west along the surface streets, careful to follow the way I'd seen my parents drive. When I got near my grandma's, it was late afternoon, and I decided to go to the park to spend the night. Several hours later it was dark and getting cold, and I was hungry. So I walked the block to my grandmother's and went to the back door and knocked.

"Oh, thank God!" she exclaimed when she opened the door. "Marcia, where have you been? How did you get here?" She gave me a big hug, and I wrapped my arms around her substantial bone-corsetted girth. She hustled me into her warm kitchen and to the tiny table, where she gave me some soup, then went down the hall to call my parents. I didn't want my mom and dad to know where I was; I wanted to stay with my grandma.

Mimi was strong, determined, unwavering, unbending, demanding. Also loving, nurturing, protective, encouraging— at least to me. She wanted me to be talented. Perhaps she saw it as a hedge against what she knew would be a harsh world for me, given the scars on my face and body. So she paid for ballet and tap dance lessons, and piano lessons from the age of five. I remember sitting on the piano bench, the kitchen timer counting down the fifteen minutes of required practice. Mom yelling out "keep going!" when I got bored and my fingers failed to plunk the keys.

My grandma brought her nineteenth-century background and beliefs into the new century with assurance and determination. She had worked as a bank teller as a young woman, didn't marry until she was twenty-eight, an old maid by any standard in the nineteen-teens. She dated two men for eight years before choosing, not the one she loved most, but the one who would let her stay in her hometown and raise what she hoped would be half a dozen children. But after giving birth to their first child, she suffered miscarriage after miscarriage, until in desperation she and my grandpa stealthily adopted my mother—a child born out of wedlock to my grandpa's younger sister—and kept it a secret for nearly fifty years.

My grandpa, a traveling salesman, wasn't home much. When he was, he escaped to his workshop in the basement. It became a family joke: Mimi would stand at the top of the stairs and call down to him, "Dick! Dick, are you down there?" And he would pretend he didn't hear.

Mimi's favorite thing to say to me was, "Marcia, you're so much prettier when you smile."

When she died at ninety-three, it was on her own terms. Her sister and her best friends were dead, my grandfather had been gone thirty years. So one day she went to bed and stopped eating. She died three days later.

She called my mom and dad that day I ran away, and when they arrived Mom was as much exasperated as relieved. I knew she was angry. I could tell by the way she held back, let my dad take over. I think she also resented that I had sought out my grandma. But she also must have felt deep terror over the possible loss of yet another child.

She must have felt I did nothing but cause trouble for her. She must have wanted to lash out, to punish me for putting them through such an ordeal. But she never said a word to me, that I recall. She left it to Dad. He hugged me close to him. He said the police had been searching for me for hours.

MOM'S COOKING

Creamed Shrimp Soup Over Rice Chex
1 can frozen shrimp soup
¾ cup milk
Quarter tsp of onion salt
Dash pepper
Half pound of cooked cleaned shrimp
4 cups Rice Chex
One quarter cup melted butter (Mom probably
used margarine)
Chives or parsley as garnish

Instructions:
In a large frying pan or electric pan, saute the Rice Chex in
butter until golden brown. Set aside. Mix cleaned shrimp
into shrimp soup along with other ingredients and warm
in a saucepan over medium heat, stirring until smooth.
Arrange Rice Chex on plates and spoon the shrimp
mixture over the top. Serve with canned peas or beans.

THIS WAS ONE OF MY FAVORITE MEALS when I was a kid. My mom didn't make it very often, so maybe that was why it seemed so special. I honestly don't remember having a canned vegetable with it, but I'm pretty sure we did since we had canned vegetables with every meal. I don't think they even make frozen shrimp soup any more, and I'm not sure I have all the ingredients correct, but I think I do.

My mom used her electric pan for a lot of things. She made Chex Mix in it around the holidays, and fried cabbage—another one of my favorites:

> *Cut one head of cabbage into thin slices. Melt one-half cup butter (or margarine) in the pan and throw in the shredded cabbage, frying until the cabbage wilts and begins to brown. Serve with fried pork chops and apple sauce.*

I wonder what happened to Mom's electric frying pan. Was it put away when she moved in with us? Later, when she moved into an assisted care facility near Molly, did it go to her? Did my sister Cher take it home to Oregon? Or did we discard it when Mom died?

Cher has Mom's old cookbook, a compilation of index cards with recipes written in Mom's distinctive script. Mom was left-handed, but was forced to learn how to write with her right hand, as was common in the 1930s, when she was in grammar school. The cookbook has recipes for Mimi's potato dumplings and egg gravy, homemade egg noodles and oxtail soup, Dear Abby's chocolate cake, Mom's pot roast (Dad's favorite), and so many other meals from our childhood.

I liked most things Mom made. Ones I didn't:

Liver and bacon (she would add onions for Dad)

Braunschweiger sandwiches

Orange Jell-O with celery and cottage cheese (awful)

Some of my favorite desserts were rhubarb pie, Dear Abby's chocolate cake, confetti angel food cake, peach and blueberry pie, and my grandma Meier's *kuchen,* a German coffee cake with cinnamon and raisins. When I got older and made *kuchen* for myself once, I was disappointed with how dry and tasteless it was and wondered if I'd gotten the recipe wrong, or if my memory was faulty.

So many questionable memories—like seeing scenes through water: blurred, shifting, inexact. Not to be trusted. But if you can't trust a memory, what can you trust? Every daily act and occurrence comes under suspicion. Did I interpret that comment correctly? That gesture? That raised eyebrow? What did that mean, what happened just now? And how might one remember and write about it?

Did Molly mean to accuse you of stealing from your parents? What could possibly have led to that, you wonder. What had she seen in Mom's filing cabinet that made her think such a thing? She said, *Mom and Dad lent you money*, but did she never see the paper that showed you paid it back?

And now you and she are screaming at each other in your parents' driveway, and your dad has just died of cancer and your mom has sold their home of thirty-five years and bought a condo when you went out of town for the weekend and she's moving in a month.

You want to smack your sister, more for the fact that she has screwed up her life than for anything else. Never mind that you've screwed up yours plenty. She has the gall to question you? You are furious, and you scream at her once more, get in your car, slam the door, and drive away.

It is dark. Pitch black. I am floating in a cool mist. As I peer into the darkness, I see the shape of a woman's body. Suddenly she sweeps toward me, fast as lightning. She has blonde hair and looks like Farrah Fawcett, I think—or perhaps my younger sister. Her arms reach out and I feel her fingers close around my throat. I start to scream. I feel someone shaking my right shoulder, and as I wake up I'm still screaming. My heart races and I am breathing hard. I sit up and look toward the end of the bed. My daughter is kneeling there, where she had fallen asleep hours before. Her face looks stricken.

"Mommy?"

"Marcia, are you okay?" John asks. "You were yelling."

I look around the bedroom. I have never experienced such a vivid and frightening dream. I was convinced I was being strangled. That I was going to die.

"I'm okay," I say, though I am shaking. "I guess it was just a bad dream."

A few days later I recounted the nightmare for Michael.

"Are you sure it looked like Farrah? Maybe it looked more like your sister."

"Why?" I ask.

"Because I'm wondering if it was, in fact, you."

"Trying to kill myself?"

"Trying to get your attention."

That dream scared me awake, after years of sleep-walking through life.

I realized I needed to make some changes.

Elizabeth Lesser, in her book *Broken Open, How Difficult Times Can Help Us Grow,* writes about the journey of the soul. She warns that if you ignore its callings, it will become increasingly insistent—it will knock you over the head with something, an interrupting event, a signal, or a dawning awareness that demands your attention.

"Your soul is always sending messages. If you regularly paint or sing or write poetry to uplifting music; or if you meditate and pray; or if you walk in nature, or move your body in sports or dance, you know what it feels like when you and your soul are in contact. *You feel a river moving in you, a joy (from Rumi)...,*" she writes.

"Yet so often we resist the pull of the river. We tune out the call of the soul. Perhaps we fear what the soul would have to say about choices we have made, habits we have formed, and decisions we are avoiding. Perhaps if we quieted down and asked the soul for direction, we would be moved to make a big change. Maybe that wild river of energy, with its longing for joy and freedom, would capsize our more prudent plans, our ambitions, our very survival...And so we shut down."

But, she warns, this is a mistake, because if we don't pay attention to the yearnings of our soul, they will become more and more insistent, like the woman in my dream. As Lesser says, "If we don't go looking for what lies beneath the surface of our lives, the soul comes looking for us."

When I was thirteen or fourteen, not long after my family moved to the suburbs, I had a crisis of faith. The disconnect I felt with the Catholic Church grew deeper as I moved into puberty. I was acutely aware of my scars and my increasingly gangly and awkward body. I longed to experience a first crush, first kiss, first boyfriend. Yet a part of me knew—with absolute certainty—that that was not available to me.

One day, distraught and searching for help, I went to our suburban church and entered a side door. It was a quiet mid-afternoon. No one was in the sanctuary, so I crept down the aisle and sat in a pew a few rows from the altar. I prayed for a sign, some symbol from God that he was real, that he existed, that he cared for me, that I could find succor in him. I sat for a long time, waiting for something...anything. Then a priest came out from behind the altar and saw me. He came toward me and asked, "Do you need something?"

I was terrified. I thought I'd get in trouble for sneaking into the church when I wasn't supposed to be there. That had been my experience of the church.

So, although I desperately wanted the priest to come and sit with me and tell me God was real, I stood up and fled.

I have always remembered the priest's words as a challenge, an accusation that I was somewhere I shouldn't be. But were they? Now I wonder if I missed an opportunity. If I had asked, would he have taken the time to talk with me? To answer the questions I hadn't fully formed in my heart?

Maybe I was afraid of what he might say. All my experiences had led me to believe myself unworthy of love, of the church, of God. And so I ran. It was the beginning of my definitively turning my back on the faith that had sustained my parents throughout their lives. Later, embracing feminism, I condemned the paternalism and theological rigidity of the Catholic faith. But the beginning was in that personal moment of assuming I would be condemned rather than welcomed in the church.

As I think about it, I realize my rejection of the church was very much a reaction to my hurtful childhood experiences of humiliation in school and church. I still couldn't say No to continual surgeries, but I could say No to the institution that embodied a lot of the pain I had suffered.

It would be many, many years before I came to understand that I had made the church stand for all my sorrow and betrayal and rejection and disempowerment, from whatever source— family, people in the community, doctors and hospitals....

EXCISION

March 1, 1963 — Surgeon's notes: Excision of hypertrophic scar surrounding previously rotated flap of left cheek, extending from left temporal area, running forward, below left lower eyelid toward the nose, then descending down laterally to the left corner of the mouth and then into neck. There, in neck scar, surrounding also previously applied skin graft covering donor site of flap. Excision of hypertrophic scar of left side of upper lip. Undermining of the flap. Plastic closure of the wound from left temple to the left corner of the mouth, leaving the wounds of upper lip and neck open for future full-thickness skin graft.

SURGICAL TRANSPLANTATION OF SKIN—skin grafting—has been around for centuries. Roman and Egyptian physicians repaired damaged ears with plastic surgery as early as the first century BCE. But an Indian surgeon named Sushruta is widely considered to be the first to successfully perform skin grafting. He started fashioning new noses from strips of flesh pivoted from the forehead. It was the first flap, which is a graft of skin that remains connected to the donor site. Sushruta also was the first to perform rhinoplasty.

Sushruta's texts about his surgical techniques were translated into Arabic and eventually found their way to Europe. In the 1400s, an Italian scientist tried reconstructing noses with a piece of skin still attached to the forearm, and a German doctor described taking skin from the back of the arm "to make a new nose for one who lacks it entirely." British doctors also began to experiment with Sushruta's techniques, and traveled to India to see rhinoplasties performed.

It wasn't until the 1820s, though, that doctors executed a successful modern skin graft. Prior to the use of anesthesia, plastic surgery was extremely painful, and until doctors started sterilizing surgical tools the risk of infection was high. Another major advance came with the introduction of antibiotics.

There are two kinds of skin grafts: flaps, which remain attached and are rotated from an adjacent area, and wholly separate grafts taken from another part of the body. With a flap, a piece of skin (called a pedicle) is left attached so blood can feed the donated skin until it grafts onto the new site. Grafts taken from another part of the body are placed onto a donor site and the surgeon connects tiny blood vessels, allowing the graft to be fed from the underlying dermis. A skin graft can be varying thicknesses, depending on the injury. A tool much like a large vegetable peeler, called a dermatome, is used to harvest the skin from one part of the body, for example the thigh, for placement elsewhere.

Dr. Kislov initially used a flap from my neck to replace my damaged cheek, then covered the hole left in my neck with a full-thickness graft from my left thigh. He took a split-thickness graft (the top two layers of skin; the epidermis and the dermis) from my right thigh to cover the left thigh donor site. Most of the grafts on my chest and stomach were split-thickness, and the scars are not as prominent as the thicker grafts.

I have three grafts on my chest, three on my stomach and hips, and two on my thighs. And, of course, the ones on my face and eyelid. This patchwork of scars has always embarrassed me. Even today, though the scars have faded significantly. Still, they are there, and I am always a little hesitant to appear in public in a bathing suit. Being intimate with someone for the first time is even harder. I have spent most of my life covering up the skin that covers me.

Richard Kislov was born in Germany to Anna and Daniel Kisielow in 1921 and studied medicine at Med Fak Der Eberhard Karls University in Tubingen, Baden Wurttemberg. A year after graduation, in 1951, he emigrated to the United States where he completed his general and surgical residencies. In 1958, he settled in Muskegon and started a private practice. He became known quickly for his precise work, his fine suturing, his ability to sculpt faces—particularly cleft palates—and reconnect severed fingers and limbs. He was gifted in the art of sculpting skin, and also later in sculpting clay to create life-size bronze figures. He loved to design gardens, and studied architecture. Though he dismissed it once when an interviewer asked about the connections between his chosen fields—surgeon, builder, designer, sculptor—it would be hard to argue that he was not an artist. The only difference was the medium in which he chose primarily to work.

On Sunday mornings after Mass, Dad would hand us each a nickel, then walk with us to "The Little Green Store" a couple of blocks away to buy candy. Once, during the week, I walked to the store by myself, and when I got there the storeowner became concerned and called the police.

"Where do you live?" the officer asked me.

"Twelve Ninety-one Fourth Street," I answered. But my lisp was so pronounced he thought I said "Forrest." So we drove up and down Forrest Avenue, several blocks east, looking for my house, until he finally realized I was saying "Fourth Street."

When the cruiser pulled into the driveway, Mom rushed out.

"Marcia Kay!" she said. "What's going on? Where have you been?" She looked at the officer, who explained what had happened. She thanked him and then, exasperated, she took me by the arm and marched me into the house.

I couldn't understand why everyone was so upset. I knew exactly where I was and where I was going.

When I was little, my father would play a game with me. He would touch my nose with his forefinger and say, "What's your name?"

"Marcia," I'd yell.

"No, I think it's Gertrude."

"No!" I'd yell, and laugh. "It's Marcia!"

"Marcia Ann?"

"NO! Marcia Kay!"

"Are you sure?"

"Yes! Marcia Kay!"

When I was very young, I was sure of who I was. There was a level of confidence, of certainty about myself that I don't feel today. Was it a result of the love I felt from my father, or simply the innocence of youth? Was its loss a result of my accident? To my experiences of what other people felt about me after that? Or just the result of growing older and wiser?

My dad always knew what to say to make me feel important, whether it was advice on school ("Ignore the boys; their comments don't matter"), life ("Be yourself and people will love you for who you are"), or career ("Work hard and don't complain. Your talent and your commitment will pay off in the end"). He was wrong about some of it, but his assured beliefs gave me the strength and resolve to keep going.

Strength—stoic, uncompromising, dutiful—is what helped me survive. It's also what has kept me in adult life from being vulnerable, from allowing someone access to my deepest emotional places, from fully experiencing love.

Who am I? I don't know. That Marcia Kay no longer exists.

Identity is so fluid, dependent on circumstance, birth order, family wealth, so many variables. My disfigured face was the only thing people outside of my family knew about me.

At St. Joe's, a school photo was taken every year. I still have the photos from first, second, third grade. Each year, the photographer said, "Turn your head to the left, sweetie."

Other than those early photos of my face taken two months after the accident, I do not have a photo that fully shows my left cheek until 1964, three years later. In that fourth-grade photo my head is slightly turned to the left, but my face is partially visible. I stare unsmiling, and the thick, scar-burdened side of my face hangs heavy in the photograph.

As I have confronted my past, I have come to realize I was not the only one who struggled with identity.

My mother did not know the secret of her birth until she was forty-eight. She grew up in Muskegon with my grandparents. Attended local public schools. Graduated from Muskegon High School and earned a degree from Michigan State University. Married my dad, the son of family friends, when she was twenty-three. But she lived most of her life without knowing who she really was.

She was born in 1925 to a woman she never met. Her birthmother was her father's younger sister. Her name was

Edith. She had gone to Hollywood to seek fame and fortune, and had come home pregnant.

As the family stories go, Edith moved to L.A. to live with her brother, Russell, an undertaker who would one day marry Lottie Pickford. In 1924, Lottie and her actress sister, Mary Pickford, were as famous for their parties as for their movies. Edith desired the glamorous life her brother wrote to her about. She wanted the parties, the travel, the cars and fancy clothes. At twenty-one, she hopped the train from Detroit to L.A. I always imagine she met him at one of Lottie's parties at Pickfair, the storied estate of Mary Pickford and her then-husband, Douglas Fairbanks. The man she met was tall, charismatic, handsome—everything a small-town Michigan girl dreamed of.

The affair lasted only as long as it took for her to miss a period.

She returned to Muskegon in disgrace and shame. Her brother and sister-in-law's offer came as salvation. Dick and Kathryn had wanted another child ever since their first, a son, had been born six years earlier. But Kathryn had miscarried several times and now, at thirty-two, had given up trying. This baby born out of wedlock, this bastard girl, this love child, would be the answer to Kathryn's prayers.

I can imagine how Edith Gillard felt standing on the sidewalk, peering up at the clapboard house in front of her. It was early March. Michigan's late winter still held the town. I picture her wearing a long brown wool coat, matching hat, and high-heeled boots more fashionable than practical in the snow and ice.

She must have hugged the tiny bundle close to her bosom, pulling the pink blanket back to gaze upon the face of her daughter. The child was only a few days old but already Edith could tell the girl she called Doris would have her lover's stunning chocolate-brown eyes, deep and cavernous, like vernal pools.

You will be happy with Dick and Kathryn, she must have thought as she re-tucked the swaddling blanket. Her parents and siblings all thought it the best plan. But how painful it must have been!

I can imagine that difficult walk through the gate in the picket fence that surrounded the front yard, crunching through the snow up the walk and the five steps to the front porch. Before she could knock, the door opened and there stood her older brother and his wife, expectant, smiling, nervous.

As the family story goes, Dick swung the door wide, crying, "Come in, come in!" Gently taking his sister by the arm, he guided her through the door and into the front hall.

"Oh my, she's so beautiful," Kathryn whispered. She reached out her arms. "May I?"

Edith allowed Kathryn to take the pink bundle from her arms. A flood of anxious emotions rolled over her. Fear, doubt, sadness, joy, relief, resentment.

"I'm thinking of moving to Detroit," Edith told Dick and Kathryn. "It might make things less…complicated. I would love it if you would send me pictures and notes. I'm her aunt, after all."

"Do you want some coffee, Edith," Dick said. "Or tea?"

Kathryn stood in the hallway holding the infant.

"No, I should go," Edith said. She turned, rushed out the door and fled down the sidewalk toward her car.

They recorded my mother's birth in the neighboring county, in Grand Haven, and changed her birth date to March 1. They named her Helen Jean, though Mimi would change her mind and later call her Patsy, short for Patricia.

I have a photo of Patsy at three, holding her little dress out with her hand, curtsying like a little doll, posing for her dance class, ballet slippers on her feet. A smart 1920s flapper hat sits jauntily on her head, a sweet doll at her feet. A yellowed clipping from the January 1, 1930, edition of The Grand Rapids Herald shows four little girls from the Thornton School of Dance in ruffled pinafores and hats. Miss Patsy Gillard, age five, is the third from the left. At twelve, Patsy smiles from a formal portrait in a flounce-sleeved dress with buttons at the neck, her dark blond curls in ringlets falling past her shoulders, a ribbon in her hair.

Patsy would have the best of everything, and reflect all that my grandmother believed she and her family represented. Social status. Accomplishment. Talent. Community standing.

They never told my mother she was adopted. But it was an open secret in Muskegon, until one day a family friend let it slip during a game of bridge. My mother was forty-eight years old. She was stunned.

When she confronted my grandmother, Mimi said she never wanted my mom to think she wasn't her own child. But it turned out that everyone knew, even my dad, who never spoke of it to her.

Later, though, Mom told me she had always suspected; that things just didn't add up.

I recently found a letter my grandfather wrote to my mom on her seventeenth birthday. Grandpa traveled extensively as a salesman for a furniture manufacturer in Muskegon. This letter was dated February 28, 1942, and was postmarked from Syracuse, NY:

"Hello my sweetheart:—

The date I wrote and then suddenly took note that there is a birthday in our family tomorrow, and my little girl reaches her seventeenth birthday. A thousand and one happy returns of the day and I hope this letter reaches you in time.

You have been a 'swell little girl', honey, well nearly perfect anyway, for seventeen years. And I hope they have been happy ones for you Pat. Mama and I have tried to make them as happy as we could in what have been a rather troubled and upset world.

There was a time when everyone struggled for a living but the times were called 'normal times' when one could see well enough into the future to make plans with some degree of certainty. If one worked hard, and good health, and planned carefully, they usually got through life all right, and there was just as good an opportunity of doing much better than average as there was of falling short of that same average.

Then came the great upheaval, a war such as the world as little dreamed could happen. It was a terrific and terrible war, lasting close to five whole years. It was some few years after the close of that war that your little soul came drifting down into this world out of somewhere that your mama and I beamed with joy. You were not much to look at, to be sure, ALL women seem to think that ALL babies are beautiful. ALL men turn their heads and smile at the absurdity of such a thought, until it is their own. And then they too see a beautiful child.

Well, young lady, you really was not so much to look at when you first dropped in on us, but you were something we wanted, something we have been praying for for a long long time, so we really did think you were 'sompan'. Mama years and years before (SHHH, even before we were married and rather shocking in those good old fashioned days) had made a alphabetical list of every imaginable female name. But we just couldn't agree at first and since we had to call you something—you can plainly see that we did not want to just call you 'baby' like you would say 'kitty' and 'doggie', not a precious little mite like you—mother for some outlandish reason started to call you Patsy. Can you imagine picking out an Irish handle like that?

But that is just what she did, and dog gone it if you still are not Patsy today. Despite the fact that I still think Helen Jean is a peachy name.

And so for seventeen years you have lived in a world which has been trying to adjust itself. And it was far from being again anything such as one might call normal, when BANG!!! another war burst upon the world and frankly it is just about impossible for us to even conceive of how much it is going to upset our lives. And this of course means your life also.

That is why I hope you have been happy these last seventeen years, as happy to be with us as we have been to have you with us. We hope that we have given you something of ourselves which will help you to be happy for the next seventeen years. And if you will realize that the most and best happiness comes from helping other people to be happy I am sure that the next seventeen years will be even happier than the first seventeen years.

And so, dear Pat, I wish you great happiness in this coming year which will see you graduating from high school, and for each and every year which will follow. I want to do all that I can to help you to be happy.

And then this little teeny weeny selfish thought creeps into my mind 'I hope and pray that you will never cease to be close, and even closer, to your (signed) Daddy, who loves you very much

R.S.V.P.

If not too late I would like to get your graduation ring for you for your birthday gift. If you will get it and let me know how much I will send you the difference between the amount and the $5.00 bill enclosed.

(signed) Daddy."

The euphemistic language he used to describe how she came to them is as obvious as it is charming. No wonder my mother wondered.

EXPOSED

March 5, 1963 — Surgeon's notes: Full-thickness skin graft of left side of upper lip using right supraclavicular area as donor site; 9 sq. inches full thickness skin graft of left side of neck using left thigh as a donor area. Closure of donor site with split-thickness skin graft obtained from the right thigh.

IT IS LATE MORNING and I am lying in the hospital bed with just a light blanket over my hospital gown when a group of white-cloaked young men walk in. The day before, Dr. Kislov had replaced the skin graft on the left side of my neck with a graft from my left thigh, which he then covered with a thinner graft from my right thigh. He had been in to check on me earlier that morning. For once, my eyes weren't bandaged so I could see his face as he peered at my dressings, adjusting here and there, poking, prodding. "Ja, good," he had said, and patted my arm.

I watch as the group of young doctors gathers around my hospital bed. They each carry a clipboard and one of them introduces himself and then turns to the others and begins to explain what was done to me. While he's talking, he pulls down the blanket and lifts up my gown to show them my bandaged thighs. They all stare at my thighs and also, I am suddenly acutely aware, my nakedness. I stare at the ceiling until, apparently satisfied, they leave my room.

I had no control over things. Not then, not anytime in my childhood. I went into the hospital when my parents said I had to. I submitted to whatever Dr. Kislov or the nurses said I had to. I did as I was told. And so when I got to the age I could say No, I said it emphatically.

When I was going off to college, I said no to any more surgeries. And I have tried to be in control ever since. It's as though my fingers are gripped tightly around this thing called my life. The prospect of not being in control is terrifying, and so I cling, and cling, and cling. Because if I don't, I might not survive.

The summer after I turned seven, I went away to camp for a week. The YWCA's Camp Emery was on Big Blue Lake just an hour or two north of Muskegon. Eating in the mess hall with dozens of kids, swimming, learning how to shoot a bow and arrow, rowing boats, singing camp songs around the campfire at night, I loved it all. I made colorful lanyards for my mom and dad, and joined the "polar bear club," which meant dipping in the frigid lake at dawn, before the rest of the camp was awake.

I wrote letters home every day, and each day I'd wait anxiously at mail call, hoping for a letter from Mom. If I didn't get a letter, I'd feel devastated, then build up hope for the next day. By the end of the week, I was deeply homesick, and wanted only to go home.

When Sunday came, my chest was fluttery with anticipation. Parents began to arrive not long after breakfast, and as the hours ticked by, I felt more and more anxious. More parents arrived, packed children and sleeping bags into cars and drove off. Still, I waited.

Where were they? Why was it taking so long to come get me? Maybe they wouldn't come. Maybe they didn't want me anymore.

Finally, they drove up, the last ones to arrive. I was so relieved I cried. My dad hugged me, laughed and touched the end of my nose.

"What are you crying about?" he said. "We're here."

Night after night in the hospital, I watched my mom leave me, walk down the long corridor toward the elevator. She'd enter, turn, then stare at me as I screamed and wept from down the hall. "Mommy! Don't leave me!" The elevator door would close, and she was gone.

Every single time, I believed I would never see her again.

What did she feel as she walked down the corridor and heard my screams?

Exhaustion. Agitation. Resentment. Grief. Surely, sadness.

Now I realize she was overwhelmed. She didn't know how to respond to the pressures she felt, so she shut down.

I felt abandoned.

And when my husband stopped touching me, when he turned away from me in bed at night, it struck at my deepest fear. He was my mother walking down that long hospital corridor.

I have never been comfortable in my body. In addition to the patchwork of scars, I am tall and gangly, my long stork-thin legs out of proportion to my trunk. My sisters were better proportioned than I, but I am flat-chested. The family joke was that we got our tiny breasts from Dad's side of the family, because Mom had a beautiful petite figure.

My long legs are from my dad, but I lack his athletic ability. In school, I did everything I could to get out of gym class, and failed at team sports. Whenever we had to play softball, I begged to play outfield, and then prayed no one would hit the ball my way. Being hit in the face with a ball—any kind of ball—was one of my deepest fears. I liked to swim, but that meant wearing a bathing suit, so I rarely swam except with close friends and family.

In my early professional life, I wore large, baggy clothing. Once, a friend gave me a sexy, ribbed, form-fitting shirt for my birthday. I tried it on, but never could bring myself to wear it. After several years, I put it in the Goodwill bag and gave it away.

It was yoga that finally changed my relationship with my body.

When I turned fifty, I started taking yoga classes with a friend. Until then, my body had been like an embarrassing relative you have to acknowledge at a party. But when I started practicing yoga, I slowly became aware of my body, its awkward curves, its strengths, its ungainly proportions. I learned to appreciate my limbs, my trunk, my hands now touched with arthritis. I realized that strength has nothing and everything to do with muscles. I learned that yoga is as much perspective on life as focus on breath and movement. I began to breathe with intention. I learned to meditate.

In important ways, yoga saved me. More than once I crumpled into sobs while holding a floor position or lying in *savasana*. Emotion would well up until I couldn't contain it. And always my yoga teacher, Sue Anne, was there, saying, *It's okay. It's okay. Just let it all come out.* I will always be grateful for the space she created for me to heal, to come to understand myself, my mother, and all the other people whose presence in my life brought both pain and joy.

The hands. The chalk. The erasers thrown.

The bruises caused by needles in small arms.

Tied to bedside. Bandaged blindness.

Mother's stony silences. Nurses saying don't cry.

Surgeon God clucking his tongue,

asking for more from a five-year-old than he had a right to ask.

Sitting in church praying for deliverance

praying for the Mother, the Virgin Mary to come down from her niche

and take my hand and walk me out of the stifling church,

the two of us dancing lightly down the front steps and across the street

to get mint chip ice cream together.

I know the darkness. I know the creeping in of sorrow and grief, the sinking down. But what of light?

The kind that seeps through frozen tree branches during a Michigan winter onto the ice pond below—still light, muted.

The rays diffused in bands of color streaming through a stained glass window, illuminating the Virgin's face in an alcove by the altar.

The kind that filters through a late afternoon doorway just before the sun dips below the horizon.

The stark white fluorescent glare that shocks as you are wheeled down a hospital corridor to the operating room.

The green light of an approaching tornado, your father's eyes trained on the sky, gazing through the kitchen window, protecting you with his watchfulness.

And the light that brings joy.

Gold-tinged light emblazoning the houses across the canyon at daybreak, morning harbinger calling us to awaken and rise.

Inky-gray mists blanketing the ocean, slowly lightening to blue.

Red-orange flames licking the logs in a vast stone fireplace, crackling and popping, spreading warmth to envelop the room.

A beloved's smile, vibrant and dazzling, making me believe, at least for the moment, that I will always be okay.

Wingtips of the red-tailed hawk swirling overhead, searching the canyon for a late-afternoon snack.

Midday slice of lightning as a storm advances over Lake Michigan, blazing across the entire sky, a crack of thunder reminding us how inconsequential we are.

Sunrise over the ocean as the fishing boats go out, the sky reversing its sunset reverie—deep red, orange, pink, golden yellow.

I know the many faces of light, its tones and depths and sorrows, its moments of high drama, its small gifts. This light welcomes me home, holds me in earth's deep embrace.

These moments fill me, remind me I am a child of God, part of a great cosmic experiment.

This light.

CREATOR

Dec. 27, 1963 — Surgeon's notes: Cheiloplasty of lower lip and excision of scar and hair-bearing skin graft of neck, creating a defect 2x3 inches.

DR. KISLOV TAKES OUT HIS BALL-POINT PEN and draws lines all around my left cheek, neck and mouth, noting where he will add a graft here, where he might excise tissue there. When he is done, he sits back and stares at my face with his wide, gap-toothed smile.

"There! Now do not wash your face, Marcia. Eh?"

He looks at my mom and she nods.

"Okay! Give me a hug." He pulls me into a great bear hug, then holds me away from him for a minute, looking at my face. I see his impish gap-toothed grin, his thick glasses, his broad cheeks. I see my tiny face reflected in his glasses. I am smiling.

"Okay," he repeats. "See you tomorrow." Then he stands and leaves the room.

Dr. Kislov was the creator god in my world as a child. Quite literally he was creating my face, and thereby my identity. He was not to be disobeyed, and could be harsh and dictatorial, but also warm and approving if I was obedient, and if his creative work on me was going well.

As the years went by, Dr. Kislov turned his talent more and more to sculpture, gaining recognition regionally and nationally. After we moved to California, my aunt sent me a newspaper clipping announcing a gallery showing of his works. In it, Dr. Kislov insists his work as a sculptor has little to do with his work as a surgeon. Yet his large bronzes are figures of real people he knew in Muskegon. One bronze called "Coheleth" is the contemplative figure of a local minister, his finger to his lips, head down as if in prayer. There is a bust of his friend Herb Kersman, and the figure of a Muskegon woman, proud and draped in a silken shroud, called "Haughty." A nine-foot-tall bronze of St. Paul commissioned by St. Paul Episcopal Church looks down upon Clay Avenue from a shallow alcove above.

Kislov told the newspaper he didn't work from sketches, preferring instead to form the clay during sittings with the subject. "After a few sittings, I can transmit the feeling I want to the model." His pieces are exceptionally expressive, the faces exquisitely formed, the hands precise and lifelike.

The term "plastic" in plastic surgery comes from the Greek *plastike*, to sculpt or model. How much difference, really, is there between crafting a face from flesh or clay?

Not long ago, I went to see an ophthalmologist. After several minutes of peering into my eyes, he asked about the scars. I explained what had happened.

"Who was the surgeon?" he asked. I told him, adding that Dr. Kislov was long retired.

The ophthalmologist pushed his chair back and gazed intently at the left side of my face. After a few moments I started to feel a little self-conscious, so I said, "He did a pretty good job, didn't he?"

Almost with wonder, the eye doctor replied: "Yes. Better than good."

I blushed. No one had ever said anything like that to me.

My husband and I separated in fall 2007, when our daughter was fifteen. I had wavered for almost two years, from the time we had first seen Michael together. I guess I kept hoping that something would change, that he would try to get help, that his depression would lift, that we would reconnect on a deep emotional level. And I worried always about how a separation would affect our daughter. But we only drifted further apart.

Kendall was devastated. After he moved out, she punished me with nasty asides and stone-faced silences as only a teenager can do. I didn't know how to explain to her what had happened to our marriage. I didn't even understand it myself.

By that time my mother was living with us, and she was beginning to struggle with serious health challenges. She was diagnosed with lymphoma in January that year, and went through six months of chemotherapy and radiation. She was convinced she was going to die, even though the doctors told her she had very good odds of beating it. She became fearful, more withdrawn.

Lymphoma often develops in people who have rheumatoid arthritis. Mom had lived with RA's severe joint pain for more than twenty years. With most cases of rheumatoid arthritis, there are periods of active disease, when the joints swell and bulge and ache, and there are periods of relief, when the condition eases. Her disease was unusual in that it had never gone into remission.

When it was first diagnosed, just before she turned sixty, it hit her hard. Things she loved to do, like knitting and sewing, became extremely painful. She could no longer run the vacuum cleaner, so Dad took over. He began to help with dinner preparations. He opened cans and jars for her. They replaced the bathroom and kitchen faucets with ones that had paddles, to make it easier for her to manipulate. They changed the handles on all the doors. The joints in her hands and feet swelled and became misshapen. She and Dad had to give up dancing, because it hurt when he took her hands. At points during those twenty years, the finger joints in her hands and both her big toes were surgically replaced.

After my father's death, we moved with her into a house in Goleta, and my husband and I became her hands. And also her ears. She had started to lose her hearing in her sixties, and by the time we moved in together she was pretty deaf. She had hearing aids, but didn't like wearing them. Most of her hearing loss was in the upper registers, so she could hear John's deeper voice fairly well, but my voice and Kendall's were lost to her. Most mornings we'd sit down at the breakfast table and I'd say: "Good morning, Mom. How are you doing?" She'd look up from her oatmeal, scowl at me and say loudly, "What?"

"Mom, put your ears in," I'd yell. She'd fish them out of her bathrobe pocket and screw them into her ears. "Okay, what did you say?"

From the time we moved in together, I tried everything to make her happy. I mediated the squabbles between her and my husband. I encouraged Kendall to be kind to her grandmother, even though Mom was often harshly critical of her.

Once, when Kendall was sixteen, Mom came upon her painting in the dining room.

"What's *that* supposed to be?" Mom said.

Kendall was wounded.

We were all wounded, hurting each other with our words and our silences.

Living in the same house, it became impossible to ignore the way Mom would smile and light up when one of my sisters or my brother came to visit, when it was so difficult for me to please her. Deep silences had become our normal way of being together.

Silences throughout breakfasts at the dining room table, throughout the day while I worked at my desk, during the slow preparations for dinner, and as we sat staring at our plates. Forced conversations. False attempts at cheerfulness. I could never understand what was wrong, what I was doing or not doing to cause the silence, the coldness, the disapproving mouth.

To some extent my mother suffered because she was an adopted child, I have come to believe. There was anger, a sense of rejection. Was that one reason she withheld her love from my daughter, who also was adopted? Or was it because she was *my* daughter? Or was it because Kendall withdrew from Mom after her grandfather died?

Kendall told me she feared Mom was going to die too. But Mom was hurt, and responded with rejection. Nothing I could say after that could heal the rift, and it intensified when Kendall became a teenager.

One evening we were sitting in front of the television after dinner.

"You know, you should make her clean her room," Mom said. "It's a pigsty in there."

"What do you mean?"

"I mean her room is a mess. Why don't you make her put away her clothes and pick things up? She's going to turn into a slob."

"Mom," I said, "she gets good grades, she's on the basketball team at school, she practices her piano without nagging. I don't care what her room looks like. Just shut the door and don't look."

I stopped and thought for a moment. It was another in a long string of criticisms.

"Do you even love her?" I asked.

She softened a little, then set her jaw. She looked down at her knitting and didn't respond.

From the time Kendall was born, it was my dad who doted on her, played with her, took her to the park and beach. It took me a long time to see it, but Mom treated Kendall the same way she treated me: distant, disapproving, cold.

But at that moment, I was still deluding myself. I refused to see it, made excuses for it, insisted the hostility toward me didn't exist.

Part of me believes she loved me as best she could. Yet there are so few times I remember tenderness. So many more times disapproval. So many more times being punished with a paddle, or a belt, or being roughly dragged back to school. When she sat with me in the hospital, she was closed off and quiet. Exhausted, emotionally removed.

Yet still I craved her presence. Needed her to be there, needed the comfort that came from knowing my mom was in the room, next to my hospital bed.

Even if she wasn't there, not really.

People who have read this book have asked, why aren't you angry? Royally pissed off at your mom, your family, the doctors and nurses, the church, the nuns? I was, at one time. It's why I struck out, misbehaved, acted out at St. Joe's. It was the only way I could voice my hurt and fear in the face of constant pain and constant exhortations to buck up, be strong.

So there was a great deal of suppressed rage. But I realized—and not so very long ago—that anger would only eat me up inside. I see no point in holding onto resentments and anger.

And I *am* strong. It's what everyone says when I manage to weather another life storm—job loss, broken relationships, deaths of those I love...heartache, sadness, grief. Deep down that little girl still struggles, still wants to cry, needs comfort. But she bucks up, she is strong.

And gradually I have come to a sense of forgiveness for all of it; forgiveness of my mom, my dad, of Dr. Kislov and the nurses. I'm still working on the church.

After Mom died and my husband and I divorced, Kendall lived with me off and on for a year after her freshman year of college. She had decided to take time off from school, so she came home and got a job in a coffee shop. It was an adjustment for me after having been alone for a year. I lived in a small two-bedroom house and since I worked at home, it seemed we were often tripping over each other.

I tried to set some rules, but Kendall ignored them. I insisted her boyfriend could not spend the night. Yet morning after morning he was there when I woke up. If she asked for something, I had a hard time denying her. She'd ask for money, and I'd initially say no, then she'd whine and cajole until I relented.

If I asked her to do something, she ignored me. If she was home while I was working, she insisted on all my attention. When she was upset, she expected me to drop everything and come to her. She'd push things until I got angry and blew up. And then I'd get mad that I let her get to me.

After a while, I went to Michael in exasperation.

"Let's try some role playing. Imagine that I'm Kendall."

I took a deep breath. "Okay."

He sat across from me, then pulled his knees into his chest and began to rock back and forth. "Mooooommmmmmm," he whined. "Mom, I need you! MOM, I NEED YOU. Come here!"

I sat paralyzed.

"Mooommmm, I NEED you. Come here, Mom. Mom!" Michael yelled.

My heart started to beat hard. I felt anxious and fearful. I couldn't say no to her. Oh my God, I thought. I can't say NO!

"Michael, I can't," I said. "I need to be there for her."

"Who wasn't there for you, Marcia?"

Contraction

Dec. 31, 1963 — Surgeon's notes: Split thickness skin graft to neck obtained from the middle of the chest.

You are sitting in the playroom on the pediatrics ward of the hospital. There is a tiny table, and the nurses have brought you lunch on a tray.

You are the only one here now, though there have been times when other kids in bandages have played with you. Your head is wrapped in gauze and you are wearing a tiny hospital gown. The food is not like Mom's. But there is always a piece of white bread in a wax-paper sleeve with a pat of butter, and that is one of your favorite things. You are buttering your bread when a nurse comes to find you.

"Come now, Marcia, we have to give you some blood."

You know what this means: being strapped down for a very long time with a needle in your arm. Your bread sticks in your throat. You do not want a transfusion.

You do not want this! You feel your throat tighten. Tears well up. But you get up from the table and take her outstretched hand.

Once, when I was in second grade, Sister made me stand in the front of the class, next to my desk, in punishment. In shame.

I started to cry. I was holding my plastic book bag, which was filled with books, across my chest, and I started to take bites out of it with my teeth. Crying, biting into my book bag, spitting the plastic pieces into the bag, over and over. I don't know how long I stood there, but it felt like an eternity.

Sister ignored me while I stood and sobbed, bit and spit.

In my dream I am running through the jungle. Hands and arms are hitting me with sticks and splayed bamboo. I am running and running and they keep striking me. I am so afraid. I want my mother.

Two nights before. A *National Geographic* special. A pride of lions and a herd of elephants forced to share a watering hole. During the day, the lions don't dare attack the elephants, but at night, the elephants can't see them. One night the lions manage to cull a baby from her mother. The baby runs and the lions chase her, jumping on her back and biting her all over while others snap their jaws at her sides. Two or three lions hang onto the baby elephant's back as she runs into the thick bush. Then the baby elephant is on the ground and the lions are tearing at her flesh.

Impermanence. The state of being transitory, ephemeral, fleeting. We are tricked into thinking life is permanent whenever things seem to stay the same.

You have a longtime home, a daily routine that seldom changes, a job that requires the same skills and actions over time, a long-term partner. But when one or several of those things is upended, either intentionally or unexpectedly, we can be thrown into an unsettling state of impermanence. And if that state remains for an extended length of time, one of two things happens: stress increases and your life feels out of control, or *acceptance* allows you to live into the changes and move into a new way of being.

Part of me longs for change, for adventure, for excitement. Another part craves sameness, security, permanence. Balance is what I now strive for—heightened interest and awareness through change, but tempered by the belief that I'm in control.

Of course you hear the Buddha laughing.

In fall 2012, I traveled to Costa Rica. My cousin offered to let me stay in her beautiful vacation home on the north Pacific coast. I went to write, to meditate, and to contemplate all the things that had happened: job losses, my mother's death, my divorce.

It was the rainy season, hot and muggy, so for the first two weeks I worked on the veranda most days and enjoyed the light rains that fell every afternoon and evening. Often I'd sit in the Jacuzzi with a glass of wine and watch the sun set over the ocean. Sometimes I walked up the beach to the tiny town of Tamarindo. Mostly, I reveled in solitude.

Like most homes in Costa Rica, my cousin's is an outdoor house. Only the kitchen and bedrooms are indoors; everything else is exposed to the ocean and the gentle winds. Outdoors comes in; indoors goes out. When it rains, everyone just shrugs and watches it come down.

I sat at the tall table in the outdoor "living room" and welcomed the rain. Small yellow birds with black masks chattered in the trees above. Words flowed like the cascading wall of water that dropped effortlessly over the edge of the pool. At that moment, my life—all time—seemed to stand still. The afternoon stretched into millennia, all my scars faded into deep understanding, all my pain dissipated in the soft, warm rain.

Often I found myself retiring to my room shortly after sunset, then crawling into bed not long after. I woke at 4:30 or 5 a.m. and wrote until 10 or 11. During the long afternoons I trekked into Tamarindo, fifteen minutes up the beach, and took long walks down the shoreline to pick up corkscrew shells.

I was a curiosity there, a single woman traveling alone. The cook at the house seemed not to know what to think of my long stay. Restaurant staff stole sideways glances when they thought I wasn't looking. They were polite, but it was clear they wondered, "Why is she alone?" After several days of driving me to various places, my guide, Olman, asked me why I hadn't come with a friend. Honestly, I hadn't even considered it. This time was for me to write, to reaffirm who I am, to be fearless, to learn to be content.

I went on a zipline canopy tour by myself. Visited the *Rincon de la Vieja* national park in the north. Traveled into the interior of Costa Rica to visit the Arenal Volcano.

Arenal is one of hundreds of volcanoes considered active in Costa Rica, but it is the only one that consistently puts on a nightly display of sputtering fire, smoke and ash, with molten lava rolling down the mountainsides like glowing Slinkys. Unfortunately, it was the rainy season, and clouds obscured the mountaintop more often than not. So I didn't see the fire, but I got to see other wonders.

Olman (*el mejor chofer!*) took me to *Puentes Colgantes de Arenal*, the Hanging Bridges of Arenal park, where a two-mile walk through the rainforest included trekking over lengthy bridges that swing hundreds of feet in the air. The next morning, we visited *Ecocentro Danaus Ecologica Reserva* at La Fortuna. There I saw and photographed an assortment of rainforest creatures. I love *los animales*, domestic and exotic, and Olman was expert at finding them even in their most camouflaged states. The venomous blue jeans dart frog (*ranita venemosa rojiazul*). Boat-billed heron. *Guatusa* (like a tiny capybara). Fleischmann's glass frog. The stunning blue morpho butterfly. Yellow-crowned euphonia. Howler and spider monkeys (*el monos negro* and *el monos arana*).

One of the things I learned there is to look closely; you will always see something you didn't notice before. Corkscrew shells scattered in the sand. Tiny fish darting in tide pools. Lilliputian hermit crabs on the volcanic rock along the shoreline, moving so slowly as to be almost imperceptible. Yet if you squatted down and looked, really looked, you would see their tiny legs sprouting from under the shell.

When I was at *Ecocentro Danaus*, I would have missed everything without Olman's trained eye. *Monos* in the treetops high above. A slow-moving *gorrobos* climbing a tree. Sloths sleeping in the tallest branches, even with binoculars appearing as nothing more than brown blobs, perhaps birds' nests or clusters of decaying foliage. Even when he took my shoulders and pointed me directly at whatever creature he wanted me to see, I still struggled to detect it. The green lizard in the ferns. The tiny bat hanging upside down inside a decaying banana leaf. The sleeping Fleischmann's glass frog (once I looked, I could see its pale eyelids closed, its sides expanding and contracting with each rapid breath). Even the bright orange-and-blue dart frog. At first my eyes just couldn't find it in the leaves Olman parted with his hands. Then, suddenly, it came into view, and I had to catch my breath with its beauty.

How often do we not see the things so plain to others? I'm beginning to realize I've spent most of my life not seeing. Not understanding. Unable to connect the dots.

It's almost as if I have spent the past seven years slowly opening my eyes. Watching my life unfold, come into stark relief, colors growing vibrant with each revelation.

Costa Rica is a beautiful country. Major roads are paved, for the most part. But many are dirt (or mud) and there doesn't seem to be any urgency to pave them. In Tamarindo, the road alternates between dirt and broken pavement, and the dirt road features great maws of potholes scattered with rocks. Still, the small taxis (mostly some kind of tiny Toyota) blast through at breakneck speed. Everyone drives all over the road, edging out into traffic without regard for oncoming cars, beeping horns that no one seems to pay any attention to. Small dogs, thin, brown or black, with tall ears and long tails, run freely across the roads and loll in the front yards of tiny, brightly painted haciendas. Horses and cattle graze on the sides of the road between the pavement and the fences, oblivious to traffic.

"In my country, the horses are on the other side of the fence," I told Olman one day as we drove, and he laughed.

People were warm and generous. Every taxi driver asked (in varying degrees of comprehensible *Ingles*) how many children I had and how old they were. Where I was from. How long I was visiting. Where I'd been. My *Espanol* was limited, but somehow we managed to communicate. Olman spoke exceptional *Ingles*, so when we went to Arenal I got a two-day *Espanol* lesson.

"*Como se dice*, What is the name of this town?" I asked.

"*Como se llama, a qui?* (How do you call this place?) o *Cuantos el nombre esta pueblo?* (What is the name of this town?)"

"*Como se dice*, I went to the Arenal Volcano and was lucky. I saw lots of animals?"

"*Yo fue volcan Arenal y tuve mucho suerte. Puede ver mucho animales.*"

"Okay*, si. Gracias.*"

I *was* lucky.

SPLIT

Sept. 23, 1965 — Surgeon's notes: Excision of scar of filtrum and left side of upper lip and excision of contracted scar of left cheek and left side of neck. Closure of wound of filtrum and left side of upper lip in linear fashion with subcuticular suture of 5-0 nylon and superficial sutures of 6-0 nylon. Two Z-plastys between left corner of mouth and upper neck, suturing of the flaps with subcuticular suture of 5-0 nylon and superficial suture of 6-0 nylon.

MY MOM ADJUSTS my little brother's tie. He is dolled up in a little brown suit, with spanking new shoes. He is probably four, which means I am six. We are at the Muskegon Junior League's Annual Fashion Show, and my eleven-year-old sister and brother are both tapped to model.

I am jealous they get to parade down the runway, which has been set up in a big beautiful room among tables laid with linens and crystal and platters of tiny sandwiches and tea. But I know I can't be part of it. Mom doesn't have to explain that my face would be too jarring, too devastating to look at, even if I was dressed in a pretty outfit from one of Muskegon's best children's stores.

Yet as I write this, as I see myself so vividly in this scene, I realize I have made it up from a photograph, a yellowed newspaper clipping that shows my mom adjusting Chuckie's tie. I never went to the fashion show; only my sister and brother went.

Once again, memory achieves some impressive sleight of hand. I want to believe I was there, watching all the ladies and children dressed up in fancy clothes. The beautiful linens and china. My grandmother most certainly would have been there, and several of my aunts, and Mom's friends from her bridge club. They all were part of the Junior League. But in truth I stayed home. Perhaps with Mrs. Medema, eating freshly baked peanut butter cookies from her blue bone china plates. I hope so.

Nothing's everlasting. Not the rabbit in the yard munching on marigolds. Not the tortoise in the vast ocean. Not the way my lover looks at me or his touch upon my skin. Not the fresh-cut hay or the breakfast tomato. The laughter that floats up from the schoolyard, or the donkey's burden of sticks. Or the times I have wished for something I can't have, like an cone of mint chip ice cream, or to hear the sound of my father's voice one more time. We are all here fleetingly. And yet, do we not live as if there were no end? As if our organs will not ultimately fail? That time has slowed to a delicious standstill, and that we have made it happen?

I was in sixth grade when my parents bought a lot in the suburbs near Lake Michigan and planned to build a house over the summer. I started begging right away. Could I *please* go to public school for seventh grade?

After what seemed like months, they relented. It was a big deal; my older sister had to endure four years of Catholic high school. The price I had to pay for being able to go to public school, my father insisted, was weekly catechism classes at our new parish in the suburbs. I agreed. Anything was better than the abuse and isolation of St. Joe's.

That summer, we spent every weekend out at the lake watching our new house go up. We had Sunday breakfast in the back yard, which was mostly sand dune. Dad would bring a griddle and make pancakes and sausage. It was a time of excitement and, for me, a break from surgeries. I had undergone fifteen operations between the ages of five and nine. Now, it had been more than two years since I had had surgery. Dr. Kislov recommended we wait, to allow me to grow and my face to heal.

The idea of moving to a new community in the suburbs, of starting a new school, was exhilarating. I was so desperate to leave St. Joe's. I believed anything would be better.

Even so, I worried about whether I would be accepted. My left upper eyelid sagged. My lower lid gaped open. My left cheek was bulky and the scars stood out. I have a tendency to develop keloid scars, which are characterized by thickened and raised scar tissue. Even today, my face and neck scars remain thick, white and rubbery.

Still, I was anxious to begin what I was convinced would be a new life away from hurtful teasing and ostracization. I enrolled at the junior high near our new house. During the first week of school, no one asked about my scars or my face. No one made snide comments. No one stared. It was like a miracle.

And as the weeks went by, I started to make friends.

I don't know how to express how much this meant to me. After six years of abuse at St. Joe's, to be able to start anew, not to be the target of cruelty, bullying and shaming by other children, or by my teachers.

I was desperately unhappy during my years at St. Joe's. I acted out, which only brought me more grief. But at the very least, the adults—nuns and priests!—might have tried to practice the compassion and wisdom of the Christ they worshipped, whose model they were committed to follow. It could not have been difficult for anyone to see what I was experiencing and try to help me. Instead, they chose to scapegoat and punish a powerless child.

Now I was in a new school. No one knew me, and no one seemed bothered by the scars on my face. It was almost as if I was given the chance to create a new identity, one that wasn't defined by scar tissue.

And I did. I was popular in high school, and throughout college as well. I felt my whole life had opened up—I could imagine a life full of friends, a career—a future!—just the way my siblings could. In college, I took every course that looked interesting—biochemistry, English lit, biology, history—until I came upon a journalism class, which led to involvement with the campus newspaper. I was smitten, and changed my major to journalism in my junior year.

There were limitations to the life I imagined, of course. I never dreamed a boy would be interested in me, and no boy ever was. Not in junior high. Not in high school. Not even in college. I had lots of friends who were boys, but I missed out on the typical rites of passage of courtship and dating.

I watched my friends with their various boyfriends. I had a huge crush on a boy in tenth grade, but he wasn't interested in me. That small rejection was enough. I never expressed interest in a boy again.

I never told anyone about my belief that love was not for me. If I had, I'm certain my mother or my friends would have told me I was being silly. But it was something I knew as certainly as I knew the sun would come up the next day. Scars equaled undesirable. And nothing that happened to me in high school or even college contradicted that belief.

I am in ninth grade, standing out in front of the school where all the cool kids hang out at lunch and smoke. I don't smoke, but I like the cool kids, and even more I like the fact that they seem to like me. Someone mentions the principal, and, showing off my cool chops, I say, "Oh, Mr. Jenkins is a goddamn motherfucker."

I have no idea why I say this. What I don't realize is the principal is standing behind me. He grabs me by the scruff of the neck and marches me back into school, into his office.

I blurt: "I'm so sorry, Mr. Jenkins!"

He threatens to call my mom. Man, I am so screwed.

"Please don't, Mr. Jenkins," I plead.

He asks me if I was smoking pot, and says he is concerned that I am hanging out with the "bad" kids.

"No, sir. I don't smoke pot." I try to sound convincing. "I'm sorry I said what I did. It won't ever happen again. I promise. Just don't call my parents."

But he does, though I don't think he mentions the pot. Still, I get grounded.

I feel bitter.

Not long after, Mom takes me to see a doctor.

I don't ask any questions. This is something I am pretty used to.

On the way, I wonder why I am going to see this new doctor. Mom doesn't tell me a thing. After only a few minutes of talking with him, I realize he is a psychiatrist.

I think, *Oh my God! My Mom has taken me to a shrink! Without telling me!* I am furious.

I clam up.

At the end of the hour, he says: "Well, I think you have a lot of anger in you, Marcia."

I laugh to myself. *No shit, Sherlock!*

I walk into the waiting room and Mom stands. Without a word she goes in to see the doctor. I am so upset I pace the office, then walk toward the door. The receptionist stops me.

This makes me angrier, but I wait. She calls the doctor. When she hangs up the phone, she says, "Okay, he says you can go."

I stomp out the door, thinking, *Fuck you! Fuck you all!*

Mom and her best friend Norma grew up together, got married the same year. Our families spent a lot of time together, especially in the summers when we would go boating with them on Muskegon Lake. As kids, we called them Aunt Norma and Uncle Bob. Later, after we moved to California and Norma was divorced and living in Hawaii, she and Mom traveled together often. They were inseparable friends.

The week before my husband and I were married in Santa Barbara, Norma and I were sitting in my parents' kitchen. She had asked Mom if she could sing at the wedding. I didn't want her to, but didn't know how to say no, to either of them. So we were chatting about what she wanted to sing. She stopped and looked at me for a moment.

"You know," she said, wistfully, "we never thought we'd see the day you were married."

John and I wed in August 1982 in Santa Barbara. I was determined to be married at my parents' church, but the parish priest was reluctant to let us marry there. He didn't like that I had asked a non-parish priest—my uncle—to officiate. And he especially didn't like that I was proposing to marry a man who had been married before.

We met with him several months before. As we sat in the monsignor's office, Father scowled.

"You can't marry in the Catholic Church. He's been married before." Father nodded toward John, but never directly addressed him. John was miffed. I felt desperate to find a way to make things work. We both felt like children called into the principal's office. The priest asked more questions. I could see John's jaw tensing as he sat stiffly in his chair. I knew he was getting angry and the priest was rude. Still, I pursued.

"Yes, I know, but she was married twice before she married John."

"What churches was she married in?" the priest asked.

John explained that his ex had been married initially in the Catholic faith. The priest seized on this news. As far as the church was concerned, Father explained, John's subsequent marriage to her was invalid. Their thirteen-year-old son wasn't discussed. John was free to marry me, the priest concluded. This odd— sadly logical—argument won the day. I wanted to be married in the church, so I overlooked the irony—the hypocrisy of it all.

Norma sang at the wedding. An awful rendition of "You'll Never Walk Alone."

I stood at the altar, with John by my side, cringing, as she sang about walking on through a storm holding your head up high.

Even my wedding was not my own.

I swallowed my embarrassment and anger and pasted on a smile.

ANESTHETIC

August 5, 1969 — Surgeon's notes: Surgery is done under local anesthetic.

I AM AWAKE. I hear the scalpel crunch as it slices through the skin under my left eye and on my left cheek near my nose. I see the blood ooze up under the knife in Dr. Kislov's eyeglasses. I close my eyes and doze.

My grandfather Meier died at the beginning of my senior year in high school, and it wasn't long before my dad made arrangements to sell his share of Meier Cleaners to my two uncles. He and Mom had been planning a move west for some time, either to California or Arizona. My sister Cherie had moved to LA after she graduated from high school, and my dad's sister and her family lived there as well. But Dad was reluctant to leave while my grandfather was still alive. After his death, it was only a matter of months before we moved.

Dad bought a small business in Santa Barbara and spent the fall there while Mom and the rest of us prepared for a Christmastime trip across the country. Shortly before Christmas, Mom and I went to see Dr. Kislov for the last time.

As usual, I sat on the examination table while Dr. Kislov peered at my face. The last surgery I had undergone was a year before, and, as he often did, he pushed his horn-rimmed glasses up on his forehead and brought his face close to mine. He leaned back and lightly smacked my left knee with his hand.

"There, Marcia! Is good, *ja*? When you are thirty-five I will give you a facelift and you will be beautiful. Now give me a hug, eh?"

You will be beautiful.

It was the last time I ever saw Dr. Kislov. But many years later, when I was in my late thirties, I took one of those weekend self-improvement seminars and they encouraged us to reach out to someone from the past with whom we felt we had unfinished business. I called Dr. Kislov.

Although I hadn't thought about him in years, the seminar had brought up some very painful memories, particularly of my mother leaving me at night when I was in my hospital crib. I felt an urgent need to talk with him.

It was a Saturday and when I called his office I got his exchange. I don't remember what I said, but somehow I convinced them I had to talk with him, and they gave me his home number.

When he answered, I barely got out, "Dr. Kislov, it's Marcia..." before I broke down in tears. I sobbed through the whole conversation, which perhaps lasted five or ten minutes. He seemed surprised and happy to hear from me, and asked me about my life. I remember I told him how much he had meant to me when I was little. I think I thanked him. But mostly I cried, and he just listened and said: "*Ja, ja*. It's good to hear from you, Marcia."

Remembering this exchange makes me teary. He represented hope and pain, sadness and conflicting, inexplicable feelings of love. He was my protector and my torturer, my savior and my accuser, my surgeon and father figure.

When we left Michigan, I never considered what it might mean never to see him again—that not seeing him would leave such a huge emotional hole in my being.

Part of me never wanted to see him again. But another part, a tender place deep in my five-year-old self, wanted him to hold my face in his big hands again, to beam at me with his gap-toothed grin, to pat my knee and laugh in the big way he did. He represented comfort and safety, a time in my life when things were predictable—terrifying, yes, but predictable.

Michael sits across from me, asks about my memories of waking up and having my hands tied to the hospital bed rails. I think about being unable to scratch my maddeningly itchy ears. My stomach clenches. The fear of waking up and not being able to see, not knowing where I am or who is nearby, rises up and envelops me.

There is a disembodied voice—my mother's, a nurse's, someone who wants to stick me and draw blood. They were all the same: distant, dreamlike, unreal. Terrifying.

"It's almost like I was abused or something," I say.

"Let's be clear, Marcia," Michael says forcefully, "you *were* abused. There is no difference between what was done to you and the trauma experienced by an abused child."

"But it was done for my own good."

"Doesn't matter. It was still abuse."

My gut twisted. How could that be? Once again I had to readjust my beliefs about what had happened, and put them into a perspective that finally made sense deep inside.

Knowing that I was in fact abused finally acknowledged my own experience, not overlaid and revised by what others thought I should feel or believe. Only what *I knew*. *My* truth.

With yoga, I learned to experience my body as something other than a vessel for trauma; it helped me embody myself. I've come to terms (mostly) with my long limbs, my small breasts, the patchwork of scars on my stomach, thighs and chest, and, increasingly, my face. But I still see every flaw, every scar from my eyelid to my chin and down my neck. I feel the rough tissue when I run my fingers over my left cheek and chest.

After John and I divorced, I waited a long time before stepping into the dating pool. It terrified me. I had never dated much, and now I was single for the first time in twenty-eight years.

Then I met a man at my high school reunion and we dated for about seven months. The first time we had sex was excruciatingly uncomfortable. But soon I came to understand that—inexplicably—he actually appreciated my body. The more he praised my figure, the more I came to enjoy the attention he gave it. I was still shy about being naked, but I began to shed some of that childhood baggage about scars and my once-awkward frame.

He helped me realize I was desirable, both sexually and intellectually. Thus began my journey back to myself, to letting my mind and body become one, to em-body myself.

My Catholic upbringing was so enmeshed with the unredeemed sadness, the trauma, the abuse at St. Joe's, that I have never been able to separate the two. Just walking into a Catholic sanctuary brings up overwhelming emotions. For years, I couldn't go to Mass without falling apart. I'd try, I'd say the words, focus on the prayers, but inevitably I would just start to cry and I'd have to leave.

I know my father was deeply disappointed and saddened that I left the church. In fact, all of us did, my sisters, my brother and I. My siblings had their own reasons. Mine are entangled with and grow out of childhood trauma.

When Kendall was three, friends invited us to join the First United Methodist Church. The senior minister was a warm and engaging man whose sermons were brilliant, thought-provoking and entertaining to boot. We found community there, elderly people who embraced our family, and younger couples who had children Kendall's age. We made good friends. I missed the ritual of a Catholic service, but I found a sense of spirituality in the new church community.

But still, I searched for something more.

I spent nearly eight years working for a small Christian college. They knew me from my newspaper days, and hired me even though I told them I did not really have a faith, that I was trying to figure it all out. Those years helped me develop an adult perspective on the Bible and the teachings of Jesus Christ, who was far more radical than most people acknowledge—the very first progressive.

Even though I came to appreciate much about Christianity, I never felt that I could embrace it fully. And now much of the dogma has been highjacked over the years by a false, politically driven agenda.

So I explore. I attended a Unitarian Universalist congregation for several years, visited Jewish temples, learned a little about the Koran and Islam, embraced the tenets of Buddhism, which of course isn't a religion but a philosophy, a practice. All of this has helped me put the pieces of my life together.

Now I have greater perspective and understanding. Faith has become more about hope, love, tolerance and forgiveness (of others and myself) and less about fear and dogma and pain. The vengeful God of my childhood has become a bright essence of acceptance and affirmation that dwells in and infuses my body.

It's been a year since my husband and I separated. Mom and I are eating lunch: bacon, lettuce and tomato sandwiches—one of her favorites. She picks up a half with her arthritic fingers, crooked and weak, takes a bite.

Out of the blue, she asks, "Do you think you and John will ever get back together?"

I shake my head. "I don't think so, Mom."

"Why? Why can't you try again? What happened?"

I have never discussed this with my mother and I'm not even sure what to say to her. First, it's really none of her business. Second, I am still trying to work out my own feelings about our relationship and what caused it to fail.

"Mom, we just don't have a relationship any more."

"Well, you know you'll never find another man."

I stare at her.

A sudden, long-suppressed rage blows up inside my chest.

"Oh, my God, Mom!"

She is shocked, I think, by my forceful response, and backs down a bit.

"Well, I just mean, you know, it will be hard to find another good man."

I stare at her, my mouth open.

"Well, I guess I was just so lucky with your dad, you know. It's hard to find someone once you're older."

I don't know how to respond. I push my chair back, take my plate to the kitchen counter and leave her sitting alone at the table.

She has jabbed a white-hot poker into the very spot I have tried to ignore, tried to keep from overwhelming me, the place that believes she is right: no other man will ever want me.

Scar Tissue

Oct. 29, 1969 — Surgeon's notes: Excess scar tissue under left eye is excised and gap closed. Additional bulk removed from left cheek. Neck scar is reduced.

IT IS MORNING. Mom and I are sitting at the dining room table, and bright sun flows through the open window behind her. The smell of jasmine sweetens the air. She has eaten the oatmeal I made for her. She has her numerous pills in her little green dish next to her glass of water, and she is taking them one by one. Her playing cards sit off to the side, ready for her morning hand of solitaire.

"What do you remember about that day," I ask her, "that day I was hit by the car?"

It has been forty-three years since that disastrous morning. Now, she is seventy-nine and struggles with her arthritis and other pains. She has pain in her upper right groin that no one can quite figure out. The doctor almost dismisses it, but she complains about it constantly. Her hands hurt, her feet hurt, her side hurts.

I do not know what to do. I am at pains to make her happy. We sit at the table in silence. She frowns.

I plead again, "Mom, can you tell me what you remember about that morning?"

I am trying to write about the accident and those early years of surgeries and hurt. But I have no recollection of that morning. My older sister remembers some of it: we have talked at length. But Mom is reluctant to talk.

"I don't remember much," she says.

"It's important to me, Mom."

She looks down at her cards.

"I was on the phone with Mimi," she says, "sitting in the front hall. I heard yelling outside, and Cherie ran in screaming."

She hesitates.

"I went in the ambulance with you to the hospital. I don't remember much else. I think I was in shock."

My mother and I have lived together for six years. When my husband and I bought a house and we all moved in together, I believed she was lonely in the wake of my father's death, and that she would welcome our company—my husband, me, and our daughter.

At first it seemed to be true. But the longer we lived together, the more I noticed how withdrawn and silent she was with me, how bright and garrulous when my sisters visited.

Now we sit in quiet tension; I yearning for words from her, she reluctant to talk.

I ask if she remembers which direction I was walking when I crossed the street. I've always believed I was coming back toward the house.

"No, you were walking the other direction, over to visit your friend who lived across the street."

"Are you sure?"

"Yes," she says.

I'm still not certain. Deep inside I know I was hit from the right side, which would mean I was coming home. I can feel it in my right shoulder, the way it refuses to relax into the ground when I am lying in savasana at the end of a yoga session. Or the way it reflexively hunches up when I am feeling threatened.

I don't know why this detail matters to me. Perhaps because I do not know where I am headed these days, so confirming a small piece of the past—a past that is riddled with hurt and sorrow—will help me right the compass.

I feel as if I am flowing in a vast river without a paddle to steer the craft away from the rocks and trees along the shore. I veer toward them, and somehow—at the last possible second—my trajectory shifts and the waters carry me away from the danger. Over and over my life has raced like this toward the rocks, then careened back to calmer waters mid-stream.

I can't seem to find the rudder.

Sitting with my mother, her beautiful face only slightly lined even at nearly eighty, I consider the silence between us.

Why? Why?

Did she always blame me? Did she harbor resentment through the years about the tectonic quake I caused in her life? The hardship I created for the family, for her?

We think we know our mothers. In our childish narcissism, we assume our parents had no existence before us, don't have lives, loves, dreams beyond us. We have trouble imagining them as a couple, once—as two people, an initial relationship that led ultimately, to our own existence. Anything that pre-dates our arrival is a blank slate, and we remember our early lives with ourselves at the center.

So how to encounter the mother you never knew, the woman who met and fell in love with the man you knew only as a father, who chose to marry him and raise a family? What do you know of her friends? Those she confided in? Those she sought out when tragedy struck? What secrets did she entrust to them? What dreams did she defer, or give up? What jealousies and regrets? What heartaches?

When she told me she never got to mourn her lost babies, what did she mean? Was she just acknowledging those buried feelings? Or did she mean she was prevented from mourning her lost sons by my own birth?

They would have been my older brothers. Would they have been protective and caring? Or combative and competitive, like my younger brother? Would they have been tall and handsome, like my dad? What color were their eyes, their hair? Only a few photos remain of the one who lived eight months. He looks exactly like the pictures of my younger brother at six months, only more like my dad around his eyes. There are no images of the other baby.

Did my mother dwell upon these things when she was alone with her thoughts? Did she consider how things might have been different if those babies had lived? Or if I had not walked into the crosswalk with my bike on that lovely summer morning in 1961? If the man in the sedan had not been blind in his left eye? If he had seen the tiny five-year-old pushing her two-wheeler across the intersection?

I wonder too. Would my parents' lives have been easier? Or just different? Would other strife have taken the place of the difficulties they did experience? Doesn't everyone face hardships?

I know my mother's key to survival was to deny her feelings. She modeled that pattern well, and I learned it well. For most of my early adulthood, I denied the fear, the deep anger and hurt, of fifteen years of surgeries, hospitalizations, taunts from schoolmates, the nuns' frequent punishments, the shame of sitting—again and again—in a darkened cloakroom. Of my mother's coldness.

Now, I try to pry the feelings from her. Perhaps I should let it be, let her feelings stay deeply buried, where they are safe and cannot bring her pain.

But I cannot leave my own feelings buried. Cannot deny the ghosts who remind me that I need to heal. I need to know. I need to understand.

She will not help. She dismisses the conversation with a terse, "I don't remember."

I gaze past her at the jasmine blooming on the fence, breathe in its exquisite scent, stand and take her bowl to the sink.

Diagnosis

October 5, 1973 — Surgeon's notes: Diagnosis: Somewhat irregular scar in left nasolabial fold extending into left side of chin with excessive fullness of cheek. Surgery: excision of 3" scar in left nasolabial fold, excision of excess of full-thickness skin graft of left side of upper lip, undermining of skin flap of reconstructed left cheek and excision of excess of fat and scar in this area. Closure of wound with subcuticular interrupted sutures of 5-0 clear nylon and continuous superficial sutures of 6-0 nylon. Several space sutures were placed, leaving long ends around the wound and bolus of cotton saturated in saline was placed over the wound and immobilized by tying long ends of sutures over it. This was done to decrease dead space underneath the operative area.

UNTIL THIS SURGERY my left cheek bulged with extra fat, tugging on the skin so the lower lid gaped open and the eye was slightly exposed. It's apparent in all the photos taken of me those years, especially the school photos, for which I refused to smile.

That poor little girl who was teased and blamed and made fun of—for whom the cloakroom was her refuge and her shame—that child wanted to strike out at the kids who persecuted her, to scream obscenities and hit them with her fists. She couldn't do that, but at least she could refuse to smile.

But Dr. Kislov carved out the excess tissue and fat, and my left cheek began to look more like my right. The sag in my eyelid wasn't as pronounced, and while I wasn't all that excited about having another surgery (as if I had any say in it), I was happy with the result.

I had friends in high school, good friends who came to visit me in my hospital room and cheered me with news from school.

And I had my horse Ginger. My dad finally bought her for me when I was fourteen, after I had begged for more than three years. He found Ginger, a fifteen-hands thoroughbred mix, for sale in a neighboring county. I had to promise to pay for her stall and food, which I eagerly agreed to do. Ginger became my best friend until we moved to California when I was eighteen.

To pay for her stall and food, I went to work for my dad at the cleaners, waiting on customers at the front counter. Saturdays throughout the year and Mondays through Fridays in the summers. As far as I was concerned, it was well worth it.

I adored that horse. Next to my dad, she was the primary reason I was able to navigate the emotional ups and downs of watching from afar as my girlfriends went through all their boyfriends. We boarded Ginger at a barn near my house in the suburbs, a part of a long-gone estate. There were eight stalls, and all of them were occupied by horses (and one pony) owned by girls my age. I spent every waking hour outside of school and work at the barn. I joined a 4-H club, and we went to horse shows on weekends. I rode Ginger every single day, often to the beach near my house, where we'd splash through Lake Michigan waves and ride through the dunes. She was a huge and healing part of my life.

I loved Ginger, and I was sad when we sold her just before we left for California. Though, if I'm honest with myself, I was also ready to move on with my life, and the idea of moving to California was exhilarating.

I don't remember ever having a vision of my life as a grown-up. Perhaps because the furthest I could see growing up was the next surgery. It wasn't until I was in high school that I started to think about a career, and since I loved horses and dogs and every other kind of animal, I thought I might want to be a veterinarian.

But our move to California changed everything, perhaps for the better. I don't know how my life would have been had I stayed in Michigan. I was planning to go to Michigan State University, my mom's alma mater, because they offered an animal technology program—a precursor to veterinary medicine. But I had no plans beyond that. I ended up at Cal Poly San Luis Obispo because it was the only option.

We moved halfway through my senior year, and when I checked with one of my new high school counselors about vet programs, UC Davis's applications were already closed. She suggested the animal science program at Cal Poly, which I discovered after I arrived on campus was actually ranch management.

I never considered leaving for another school—I really loved Cal Poly and my new roommates. And after my first year I had fallen in love with San Luis Obispo, as well. It was only 90 miles from Santa Barbara, so I could go home on weekends if I wanted. And I grew to adore the aggie esthetic (and looking at all the cute cowboys from the Valley). So for nearly three years I took whatever class looked interesting. I enrolled in several literature classes, and took biochemistry, bio and organic chemistry (during which I realized that science was not my forte). Math boggled my mind. I liked sociology and philosophy, and thought about taking the Bible-as-Literature class. But my experience with pushy Jesus freaks in high school, not to mention my horrendous Catholic upbringing, stopped me from signing up.

I was so certain of things then—a budding feminist who rejected the idea of ever having children, who wanted a career, who believed we are stronger together than divided, and that the Republican Party was misguided (which turned out to be prescient). Ronald Reagan was elected president two years after I graduated from college, which presaged the dismantling of everything I believed in: the responsibility we all hold for those less fortunate—the poor, the disabled, the "others" among us.

I didn't work very hard in college until it mattered: when I discovered journalism in my junior year. It opened up a vast world for me. I began writing for the campus newspaper, and felt like I'd found my tribe. Chelsea, my 80-pound Malamute-Shepherd-mix, and I became fixtures in the newsroom when I wasn't in class. When I opened the door to the graphic arts building, she would bound up the stairs and be the first into the newsroom to announce our arrival.

My very first story for the paper was about dogs on campus, because, well, Chelsea went to school with me every day. If one of my professors wouldn't let her stay in the classroom, she'd wait for me just outside the building doors. I was under the impression that she dutifully waited there the whole time I was in class, but one day I came out early and she was nowhere to be found. At exactly the top of the hour, when class would normally end, she showed up. I have no idea where she went during class hours, but after that I either left her home or only brought her when I knew she could be in class with me.

Lorna Bevier, my first roommate, became a close friend and we ended up living together the rest of our time at Cal Poly, though in several different houses over those years. We met Lisa Heilman the following year when she became our roommate in a house in Los Osos, a tiny burg on the ocean about eight miles from SLO. The three of us lived together the rest of the time we were at Poly and remained friends for many years after.

When I graduated, I was lucky to land a reporting job with a newspaper in Camarillo, between Santa Barbara and Los Angeles, beginning a twenty-year career in newspapering that found me interviewing governors and celebrities, flying in a huge corporate helicopter out to an oil platform in the Santa Barbara Channel, and soaring in a glider plane through a silent sky over Northern California valleys. It opened me up in ways I am only now beginning to appreciate.

I am home from college for Christmas. We have gone to Mass at the Catholic church my parents joined soon after moving to Santa Barbara. Mom sings in the choir; Dad sometimes helps out with the readings. But this Christmas Eve, Dad and I are sitting together with my sister, Cherie.

As we sit down, I feel the familiar knot in my stomach begin to coil. The opening song begins, and I try to open my mouth, but the words strangle in my throat. I feel the tears come, and I have to choke back small sobs. I try not to let Dad see, but he knows. I reach for my tissue packet, and dab at my eyes for a few moments, then excuse myself to flee to the back of the church and fresh air.

I am not sure why I have this reaction every time I go to Mass, but it affirms my decision to stop going to church unless I absolutely have to, and Christmas Eve is one of those times. When Mass is over, I heave a sigh of relief—I won't have to do this again until at least Easter, and maybe if I work it right, next Christmas.

By early 2008, I was struggling. Separation, financial losses tied to the Santa Barbara Writers Conference, which I bought in 2004, my mother's declining health—I tried to control it all, holding things so tightly that I couldn't see I was headed for disaster.

When my brother was diagnosed with schizophrenia, I was the one who got the rest of the family into counseling. I was the one who joined the Santa Barbara Mental Health Association board to learn more and advocate for those who suffered from the disease. I wrote columns for the newspaper about mental illness.

When my dad was diagnosed with cancer, I was the one who took him to appointments, did Internet searches about lung cancer and possible prognoses. The night he died, I was the one who sat with him throughout the night, unable to leave his side. Always my mother lingered like a ghost on the sidelines.

Again I wonder. Did she choose to be on the sidelines, or was she there because I pushed her out?

After my dad died, I took responsibility for Mom. It wasn't even a conscious decision. My sisters lived out of town; who else would take care of her? When she, my husband, Kendall and I all moved in together, it was because I wanted it to happen. Everyone else just went along.

Once I was in a car accident on the freeway. It was raining and slick. As I accelerated onto the highway from an onramp, one of the cars ahead fishtailed, causing several others to veer and hit each other. I slammed on my brakes, but hit the car in front of me, then was struck from behind. All told, seven cars were involved. Fortunately, there were no injuries and we all managed to get our cars over to the side of the freeway.

As soon as I parked, I jumped out of my car and ran up and down the line of cars checking to see if everyone was okay. It seemed the most natural thing to do. As I think back, I realize I was the only one who did that. Everyone else either stayed in the car or stood quietly on the edge of the freeway, waiting for the Highway Patrol.

Michael asks, "Why do you think you have taken on responsibilities that aren't yours?"

Honestly, I don't have a clue. Then I think, *Maybe I'm atoning.*

I bought the Santa Barbara Writers Conference in 2004, at a time when it was stagnating. I worked to bring in new workshop leaders and fresh speakers, but I lost a lot of money. With conference losses mounting in spring 2008, I realized I had to find another job. A friend of mine told me about a writing position at the University of California, Santa Barbara. I applied and got the job, but within weeks I realized it wasn't right.

After having been my own boss for years, the experience of sitting at a desk from 8 to 5, required to check in and out on a whiteboard, being overseen and managed to within an inch of my life, was just untenable. I knew I had to create something different, but I also couldn't give up a salary that for the first time in several years meant we could pay our bills.

That fall, the U.S. and global economies took nose-dives and I put the writers conference on hiatus for the following year. Other conferences did the same; in fact, a number went under entirely. It was a crushing blow.

Meanwhile, Mom seemed to be worsening. She'd forget how many pain pills she'd taken, and so she would take more.

She fell in the middle of the night, twice requiring visits to the emergency room. Once, she pitched into a table in the dining room, and the next morning her face looked like she'd gone four rounds with Mohammed Ali.

I took her Vicodin away from her, and she was furious with me. How dare I take her pills? She insisted she could handle them herself. But then I noticed she couldn't track our conversation, or she'd sit almost comatose in her chair for hours.

Dementia began to steal her memory and much of her personality. I hired a caregiver to help her get dressed and make sure she took the right medications at the right time. She started to forget to feed her beloved cat. She snapped at me and Kendall. She didn't know the nieces and nephews who wrote her cards at Christmas. She seemed to be in constant pain.

I took her to the doctor.

"Isn't there anything you can do for her?" I asked.

He suggested a new medication, but it only added to her befuddlement.

One afternoon, as I helped her to bed for a nap, I thought I detected a strong body odor.

"Mom, when's the last time you took a bath?"

"I don't know, a few days ago."

"Let's get you in the bath now," I said.

But she refused. The next day, with the help of her caregiver, we got her into the tub and washed her hair.

I was exhausted, emotionally and physically, and I was wracked with worry about Mom, the conference...about everything. So I called Cherie and asked her to come down for a couple of weeks over Christmas to help. After a week of waking up with Mom at all hours of the night, Cher agreed we needed to find an assisted care facility for her.

Two weeks later, in January 2009, John was laid off. Even though we were separated, we still shared expenses. I panicked. How would we pay our mortgage? How would we pay our bills? How would we survive?

What about Mom?

ABANDONED

Nov. 15, 1973 — Surgeon's notes: Diagnosis: Lip deformity with notching of vermilion. Surgery: Revision of shape of entire lower lip, resection of triangular scar just below the vermilion of the lip, resection of notching of the vermilion in the area of the scar, advancement of lateral and medial portion of the lip and suturing of muscular layer with interrupted 5-0 nylon sutures and suturing of skin with subcuticular sutures of 5-0 clear nylon and continuous superficial sutures of 6-0 nylon. Repair of mucous membrane in vermilion with interrupted parallel mattress sutures of 5-0 nylon.

THE LAST TIME I SAW MY MOTHER she was lying on her bed, grasping her hands over her chest, fretful, her head upon the pillow. Her Siamese cat curled up by her knees.

"It's okay," I said as I bent down to kiss her cheek lightly. "You have Lora Su right here. Molly will come in the morning. It'll be okay."

It was my first visit since my sisters and I moved her to a facility in San Luis Obispo, near Molly.

She had lived with me for nearly eight years. When we moved into the house together, she joked: "I'm not moving again. They'll have to take me out feet first."

Over the years, I repeatedly promised her I would never send her to a nursing home. She feared it. Especially when her health began to decline.

That Christmas when Cher came to help, Mom started to complain of very severe pain, so much so that we took her to the emergency room on Christmas Day. She was in and out of the hospital for the next three weeks. But they couldn't find anything wrong.

When we finally decided to find a care facility for her, I felt guilty and heartbroken, but so overextended and distraught I knew I couldn't do it any longer. Then I faced the task of finding the right place. I tried to explain to her that we needed to find somewhere she could be safe and cared for.

"Why can't I stay here?" she pleaded.

"Mom, I can't take care of you by myself any more."

I visited more than a half-dozen homes. They were sad places, for the most part, whose residents sat in wheelchairs and stared into space. One I toured seemed full of happy people, with loving caregivers. It was a large house in downtown Santa Barbara, but the place was worn and dingy and she would have had to share a room with another resident. The cost would have been almost $4,000 a month. As I walked through the house, I was overcome, and sat down on a couch and cried.

Molly finally found a place in San Luis Obispo. It was lovely and cheery, with a competent and caring staff. I took Mom up to tour the facility, and while we were enjoying lunch, I asked what she thought.

"I don't like it," she said. "This place is for old people." She had just turned eighty-four. It was a nice place and we could afford it. Molly wanted her close. So we signed the contract and moved her there in late March. Cherie and her husband came down to help. It was a hard day. Mom kept asking why we were packing her things. Repeatedly, I sat down at her feet as she sat in her chair, wringing her hands, and explained that we were moving her to an assisted-care facility near Molly. All of us were in tears.

We drove her north with her furniture and her cat, and moved her into her tiny one-room apartment. She was unsettled. Molly spent the first couple of nights with her, then visited several times a day.

Repeatedly she asked, "When can I go home?"

Two weeks after the move, I drove up to take her to lunch. It was a Sunday, and she seemed happy to see me. After lunch I stayed and watched as she played games with the staff and some of the other residents. She seemed to enjoy the time, but when she tired we went back to her room. I stayed for a short while, then said I had to go.

"You can't stay?" she asked. "I don't want you to go."

She lay down on her bed.

"I know, Mom, but I have to go home. Lora Su's right here. Molly will be here tomorrow."

I smiled and tried to reassure her. I kissed her cheek and headed toward the door. I glanced back.

She looked at me, her mouth a sadness I could not touch. Her eyes said *do not abandon me*. It was a familiar place, a place I had inhabited for so many years when I watched her repeatedly leave my hospital room and walk down a long corridor to the elevator.

Two days later, my sister called to say Mom had been taken to the hospital the night before. The staff had found her unresponsive. She was resting, but very ill, the doctors said. For the next four days Molly reported on her condition. She was always upbeat. Mom was sick but things were looking good.

Early Saturday morning, she called to say she had been to see Mom and she was cheery and much better.

I got into the shower, confident Mom was on the mend.

An hour later, Cherie called. "Mom is gone."

Molly had barely arrived home when the hospital called to say Mom had passed away.

"It's not your fault," Cherie said.

Cherie flew down from Oregon the day after Mom died, and we began to plan her memorial service. Despite our Catholic roots, we decided to do a simple, non-denominational memorial in a park not far from our house. Mom left no specific direction for a funeral, so we prepared a memorial that would be meaningful for us.

We reserved a section of the park, created a poster board with pictures of Mom with all of her children and other family members, prepared ham sandwiches and bought soft drinks, wine and sparkling water.

I felt disconnected—numb and distant, as if I were sleepwalking through the days. In truth, I had a sense of relief. Overwhelming, all-encompassing, embarrassing relief.

When our friends and family gathered in the park, my siblings each stood up to offer remembrances of Mom. My sisters spoke eloquently of her, her graciousness, her love, her selflessness. My sister's stepson got up and talked about how she had embraced him as part of the family. A longtime friend of Cher's said Mom was the epitome of motherhood—loving, giving, warm.

As I listened, I thought, *That is not the woman I knew. Not the mother I experienced.*

When it was my turn, I read a poem, "The Place I Want to Get Back To," by Mary Oliver. The last lines are

> Such gifts, bestowed,
>
> can't be repeated.
>
> If you want to talk about this
>
> come to visit. I live in the house
>
> near the corner, which I have named
>
> Gratitude.

A Final Suture

June 24, 1976 — Surgeon's notes: Resection and repair of the triangular scar below lower lip. Placement of a surgical steel suture in the upper left cheekbone to hold skin and reduce cheek sag.

I was done. That's what I told my parents after that last surgery. I never wanted any of the surgeries, but I did what my parents told me. And so, after we moved to Santa Barbara they consulted a surgeon there. It may even have been at Dr. Kislov's encouragement. They didn't tell me. They didn't ask me my opinion on any of it.

That last surgery actually led to my looking far more normal. The surgical steel suture still holds my left cheek up so that it matches my right cheek. It's tender, even after all these years, but it works. The surgeon excised the jagged triangle of scar tissue from my lower lip, and told me not to smile or stretch it in the days following surgery. But friends came by to visit and we laughed and laughed. The next week, when the surgeon peeled back the dressing and looked, the new lip scar was stretched, ruined.

She was angry, but I didn't care.

Only two times I disregarded my surgeon's instructions. When I stood and jumped in my crib after Dr. Kislov told me to lie quietly, and I had to suffer the humiliation of being blinded once again with bandages. And in California, when I didn't care that the new scar on my lip was stretched by laughter.

There were many more times I wanted to disobey, but was too young, or too afraid, or too powerless to do so. I was raised to respect authority, but I was desperate to have some small smidgen of control. In a way I was saying to my parents and the surgeons: I don't care; I have the final say; I get to determine my destiny, my looks, my life.

I wanted control, and I took it, even if it meant sabotaging myself.

In June 2009, two months after Mom died, my husband and I filed for bankruptcy. I was told to leave the writers conference alone. People who had pre-paid for the 2009 conference and others who had signed up for our March poetry conference lost their money.

I felt awful. I felt worse than awful. I couldn't sleep. I was always on the verge of tears. I felt that familiar, desperate twist of anxiety and fear in the pit of my stomach.

I made so many mistakes. Stupid mistakes—honest mistakes—but mistakes nonetheless.

People were angry with me. Really angry.

Nothing in my life had ever seemed as bleak. I was physically exhausted, emotionally spent. I just wanted it to all go away, and I didn't see a way out.

In a brief dark moment, I thought of killing myself. Then I knew I could never do that to my daughter. Still, I had reached a place where suicide seemed a viable escape. And that scared me as much as the straits I was in.

A year after Mom died, Kendall graduated from high school. During the last six months of her senior year, John had moved back into the house, into Mom's old bedroom, to save money. We had been separated almost three years, and within months I knew I wanted a divorce. I think Kendall held out hope all those years that we might get back together. I don't know why I hesitated to file. I think being alone terrified me at some deep level. But after he moved back into the house it became clear to me, finally, that our relationship was over.

At the same time, editing and coaching other writers was providing enough money that I thought I could leave the job at UCSB. It felt a bit like stepping off the ledge of a tall building, but I had prepared, found an affordable health care policy to cover me and Kendall, made a realistic budget based on my freelance earnings, taught writing workshops to bring in extra money.

I enrolled in an MFA program, which began a new unfolding of my intellectual life. During that time, I discovered a new serenity. I would wake and think, read and contemplate, write and ponder. I rarely watched TV or listened to the radio. I simply sat and thought.

What does it mean to stop and just…consider? Sometimes I sit at my desk and stare out the window. When I did that as a child I was reprimanded. But now it opens up opportunity for discovery. Daydreams reveal old memories and foster new understanding. I relish the time that has come into my life.

My mother comes to me in fragments. Or as an extension of my father. But never as a whole person. Only a disembodied voice, or a hand reaching through the crib bars. Then in retribution for some slight, a sharp paddle on my backside, or a swift jerk on my arm, or a disdainful look. She comes to me as silence. Rejection.

I did not see it until my dad died. I was forty-three, and suddenly all her coldness flooded in with overwhelming clarity. I had thought she was lonely. Over time, I realized she had always been that way...with me.

But I could not allow myself to see it, could not believe it. So I dismissed—compartmentalized—my experience of her.

All those years, after all, I had my dad.

No one else acknowledged her distance, her coldness with me, so I must not be experiencing it.

I could not trust myself, anyway. If I was afraid, they had all said, "There's nothing to be afraid of." If it hurt, they had all said, "It doesn't hurt that much." If I cried, they had all said, "There's nothing to cry about." So why would I put credence in what my own eyes, my own heart, told me?

I shut away the hostility, the harshness, the emotional withdrawal, the anger she directed at me. The inexplicable dislike.

My earliest memories I locked away in a place called Sadness. Then I made up a different story to cling to.

I am good at making up stories. I've made a career of it. But there are some things I know intuitively. Like the fact that I was walking home from my friend's house when I was hit by the car. My mother had a different belief, which I have honored in the retelling at the beginning of this book, primarily because that was the story I was told. When I asked her much later, my sister remembered a third scenario: that I was walking in another part of the intersection.

My body tells me the truth. My shoulder tells me the car hit me from the right side, which means I was coming home from the other side of the street. I have no doubts.

Of course, I was traumatized, and trauma alters one's reality. Throughout the writing of this memoir, I have been surprised to discover that something I believed in my deepest soul may not have been true. How often do we trust our memories, and find that we didn't know the truth of it after all?

But all these years later, I only trust in the one thing that recorded the trauma—my cells, my body—and realize that while I may not know the "facts," I know the truth.

Not long ago I was unpacking several boxes of photo albums that had been in storage since we sold our house in Goleta. As I was sorting through the photos, I came across one of my mother taken in Grass Valley, right after I got my second newspaper job. It was 1979. Mom had come to help me settle into the little house I rented for my dog Chelsea and me.

In the image she is sitting on the front steps with her arms around the dog, wearing jeans and a sweater shawl, her dark hair short and curly. Her petite figure is trim, and there is a wide smile on her face. She was fifty-four in the photo, just two years younger than I am at this writing. It struck me, then, how much I look like her today. More than either of my sisters. Our faces have the same roundness, the same deep brown eyes and brows, the same nose, the same smile. I sat and stared at the photo for a long time, my throat tightening with regret. I started to weep.

After Dad died, Mom and I occasionally went to the cemetery, and always on Memorial Day. I would clip flowers from the garden—white iceberg roses, jasmine, lavender, calla lilies, some green ferns—carefully placing them in a plastic bag with a wet paper towel to keep them fresh for the drive.

Dad's chamber in the mausoleum is high up on the wall, perhaps ten feet up, so you have to crane your neck to read his name and the inscription Mom chose: Dancing Together Forever. After placing the flowers next to his name with a tall pole, I would sit down with Mom on the low wall in the middle of the courtyard. A pall would fall over us as we peered up at the plaque. Sometimes, one of us would say, "I miss him." And the other would nod. A few tears would fall. After ten minutes or so, Mom would say, "Okay, let's go."

We'd drive home in suffocating silence.

Now, when I go to the cemetery, I visit both of them. I take white roses and jasmine and lavender and ferns, and I sit on the low wall and think about grief, and blame, and love, and forgiveness.

I often think about my dad. How much I miss him. How much I wish he could have been here these past years to give me his advice, his love, his support. With my mom, he would have said, "She loves you." And maybe from his perspective that would be true. With the conference, he would have very early on said, "Don't buy it; it's too risky." With John, he would have said, "You made a commitment, stick with it." And all of those things were the opposite of what I wanted and needed to hear.

I think about my mom, about her lost babies. I think about the surgeries. Dr. Kislov's masked face bathed in operating room light. My hands tied to hospital bed rails.

I think about standing by my desk biting into my plastic book bag and spitting the pieces into the bag. About the dark, wet wool-scented cloakroom. I think about the words in my head:

"We never thought we'd see the day you were married."

"When you're thirty-five I'll give you a facelift and you'll be beautiful."

"We told you never to cross the street without looking."

I lie down on the floor at Michael's. Like the day I sat on the storage room cement, and when I sat on the floor to look at the old photographs, I need the stability of the ground below me. Mountains of grief swell inside. I let the sadness flood through me. Feel the welling emotion in my back and chest. Tears flow down my cheeks and throat and pool on the floor below my neck.

Finally, I whisper to my mother: "Take it back. Take it back. Your grief is yours to carry, not mine. I have my own to bear."

And the deep penetrating ache in my lower back vanishes.

Sunday Mornings

When I was a little girl my dad would hold my hand when we walked to Mass on Sunday mornings. Down the block, past Mrs. Donohue's house with the tulips, past my cousins' house with the big swing on the porch. Past the rectory and the school and the convent to St. Joe's.

All of these things are gone. My dad, the church, the tulips. My little sister.

I am awash in grief, and I don't know how to swim out of it. I can't seem to right myself, even amid all these good things in my life. My daughter, a new beau, travel, my friends, my sweet dog, who never worries about yesterday or tomorrow.

I know I have to face a truth that I have been trying to avoid.

I have to live my own life. I have to take care of myself. I have to rely on my own self, and not depend on someone else.

I had started to fall for the fantasy that someone else would take care of me. Just a little, bit by bit, I allowed it to creep up on me.

Now I realize, again, that fantasies are always false. They don't exist, or they exact a horrific price.

How many times do I have to learn this lesson? Many times, apparently. Yet, and yet…where is the mutual trust, the interdependence that works for good? For we are all dependent on each other, and loneliness bound up in self-reliance can be deadly.

How to balance, then? How to find that place where you know and trust someone will be there and you can depend on that, but also never lose yourself?

I do know this: This grief, this sadness, this sorrow, is no friend. It lies down on the bed beside me and holds me so tight sometimes I cannot breathe.

A Buddhist friend once told me about a dream. He was a martial artist, and in the dream, he was surrounded by eight terrible warriors advancing on him with weapons. He frantically tried to figure out how he could take them on— one by one? Two at a time? It would be impossible. Finally, he sat down in the middle of the circle, turned inward and started to pray. Instantly, the warriors turned to angels, beings who surrounded him with love and kindness. The message, of course, is to stop struggling.

DR. KISLOV

Dear Dr. Kislov,

I hope this finds you well! I'm sure you remember me: You were my surgeon from the time I was hit by a car at age five, in 1961, until we moved to California in 1974. I am writing a memoir, and would love to have a chance to talk with you.

If I come to Michigan sometime in the next few months, would you be willing to meet with me? Do you still have any records from all those years ago? My dad kept invoices from most of my surgeries. If I brought them, would you be able to tell me in more detail exactly what was done? I'd also love to talk with you about anything you remember about the day I was injured. My family has told me stories about Bill Bonds, our family doctor, asking you to see me after I was brought in, but I don't know if it's true. I also was told you happened to be at the hospital when I arrived, but I don't know if that's true. I know you were living in Grand Rapids at the time.

I don't know for certain right now when I will be coming, but I'm hoping sometime in February, if not before.

I look forward to hearing from you.

With best wishes,

Marcia Meier

I never heard from him. There were so many questions I wanted to ask him. What did he think when he first saw me in the emergency room? How did he plan the surgeries over all those years? Did he have a grand scheme in mind all along, or did he make it up as time went by, adjusting for this result or that?

Did he care for me at all?

Dr. Kislov died in November 2012. He was ninety-one. My cousin sent me the obituary from The Muskegon Chronicle, which said he was known as "a skilled surgeon, a sculptor, a lay architect, a landscaper and pond designer, and as a great lover of nature." I was struck by the comments left on the funeral home's website; there were others—other children—who knew him in the same way I had.

A woman from Traverse City wrote: "Your father was a huge influence in my life. At age thirteen I walked into your dad's office in North Muskegon. I sat anxiously with my parents waiting to see if he could help me. There was a man sitting next to me. He probably saw the anticipation and fear in me, and said, 'he can do anything, just trust him.' I met him a few minutes later. He seemed like a giant to me. He smiled, peered intently into my face and then looked right into my eyes and said, 'I can do dis.' It took many surgeries and many years, but he kept his promise and I kept mine, which was to trust him. He brought so much to my life and taught me the true meaning of seeing someone for who they are, not what they look like."

A couple from Twin Lake, Mich., wrote: "Our son was home from Chicago the other day and I looked at him and thought of you, Dr. Kislov! Thirty-six years ago we met at Hackley Hospital. You were called in to see our son, who was born with a cleft lip and palate. You took one look at him and said, 'I will make him beautiful!' and you did!"

Many others wrote similar tributes.

And he told several of them, as he did me, that he would make us beautiful. Such an interesting thing to say to a child. I remember thinking at the time that being beautiful wasn't something I ever thought about. I just wanted to look normal. To him, though, it was the greatest gift he could offer.

Here's something I know: My face is not only a face. I can see it in my mind's eye. And I can't, because when I look in the mirror, the face I see is not mine. It's something I made up, something I created to hold my childhood fears, a vessel for sadness and hurt, a place for momentary and long-lasting loss. Skin and bones and gristle and scar tissue that rises and flows, pink ridges of grief laid bare. Raw. Then I look again. And it is simply a mouth, a nose, deep brown eyes, cheeks, chin.

Change is the only constant. If you resist, you suffer. And all suffering, as the Buddha says, is unnecessary. Allow. Allow for renewal, re-creation, movement. Do not be dissatisfied with what occurs; it will soon enough transform into something else, and it is up to you to decide how to experience it.

We are all creatures of habit, but habit never serves one's soul. I want to allow, to be, to remember that this moment's surprise, or judgment, or consternation, is quickly replaced with the next moment, and the next. When we hold onto a particular moment, even as it disappears, we grasp at wisps of smoke. Gone, ephemeral essence lost in the moment of passing time.

The challenge is to accept what comes and make it your own revelation of the God within. Life is creation; it is only our egos, our ever-fertile minds, which deny and bargain for it not to be. God's plan is unknown, but since you are God, you get to create the plan. But remember, other souls are creating their realities as well. We cannot know all the plans, only create our own. Which depend on our own responses to the events that occur around us.

There is always a time and place for grief, for remembering loved ones who have left us, and for embracing the new self that loss is creating in us. Acceptance is so difficult, and yet liberating. We know the God within us and within them remains.

I know my father surrounds and guides me. It comforts me, and I can almost forgive God (and him) for "leaving" me. I must choose to accept this new form, the essence that remains, and take comfort in that reality.

Have I found myself? No. Not completely. But I'm more aware of my whole self, my body, my face, and the roles they all play in my perception of who I am.

What does it mean to find oneself? For me, it has meant pulling all my splintered pieces together and understanding how that splintering affected me. It feels like the end of a very long, difficult journey. But who can know what life will bring? Being aware means I can make different choices. Choices based on what's in front of me and not on what happened five decades ago. I can choose to follow my own heart and not be swayed by what others might think of me.

I can choose to see my face as a work of art, because in ways most people can't claim, it is. It is one of Dr. Kislov's sculptures, crafted with scalpel and sutures and surgical steel.

I am not my face.

And I am.

Home Again

We drive past the house where I grew up. It looks the same, although someone has renovated it. It has a more modern roofline and the porch has been enclosed. It's painted soft beige, with white windows, instead of the gray siding I remember. I turn around to look back at it.

"Is this where it happened?" my boyfriend asks as we near the corner.

"Yes," I say. "That's where the man stopped the car, in front of our house. He had to back the car away so they could get me and the bike out from under."

My daughter, in the back seat, draws in a quick breath.

"It looks almost the same," I say. "And that's Mrs. Medema's apartment building next door."

We are in Muskegon for the funeral of my Uncle Bud, my dad's last remaining brother, who has just died at ninety-three.

That morning, I saw most of my twenty-eight cousins for the first time in more than forty years. Joe, my younger brother's best friend growing up. Joanne and Barb, my older sister's best buddies. Danny, my second-oldest cousin. We had spread all over the country, some were on second spouses, and there were dozens of grandchildren between us. Only one of us had died: my younger sister, Molly, just a few months before.

191

My boyfriend, my daughter, Kendall, and I represented my father's family, who left Michigan for California in the mid-'70s.

"Drive around the corner," I say to my boyfriend.

He turns left and drives down the street. The neighborhood looks strangely denuded. I remember leafy trees—maples, oaks, birches. Somehow it feels empty, the street and curbs crumbling. The front yards are dirt, where my memory wants green lawns.

"There's Bolt's Hardware," I say, pointing to a squat storefront on the right.

The sign still hangs in front, but the windows are boarded and it appears to have been turned into a now-closed antique store.

"I used to come over and sit with Mr. Bolt in his office overlooking the store and talk with him as he did his books and smoked his cigars."

I gaze at the peeling façade.

"Turn right up here and drive up a couple of blocks. I want to see the church," I say.

We head north toward downtown. Just two blocks up should have been St. Joseph's Catholic Church, where we went to Mass every Sunday, and where my siblings and I went to school. I had heard it was closed. But it's gone. Where the church and school once stood is a sprawling senior center surrounded by a pleasant-looking fence and spacious parking lot. As I look, I struggle to re-imagine the old stone church and brick school. Where exactly had the church stood? I knew it was on the corner, but was the front door on this street? And what of the rectory, the convent and the school? All gone.

We circle back toward Fourth Street and the house.

As we pause in front of it, I look around once again. I imagine Mrs. Medema out in front of her building watering her flowers. I remember the bully Pauly Schmidt, who lived behind us down the alley. I hear the echoes of kids playing kick the can and my mom's voice calling us into dinner as the summer sun set.

My boyfriend asks how it feels to be there, to be at the corner where it happened.

Nothing. I feel nothing.

Then it occurs to me that perhaps because I went on living in that house, near that corner, it would have been unbearable to imbue the house with the trauma. Instead, I gave the trauma to the church.

At the funeral Mass, we are surrounded by my cousins and other family and friends. I look up at the cross above the altar, and feel the familiar tightening in my throat. Tears sting my eyes and I have to take a deep breath. I breathe out, breathe in again, gulping for air, holding back the sobs that threaten to overcome me. But this time, as I struggle with the emotion, I begin to feel a sense of peace from deep inside.

I look at the songbook as we begin to sing. I think of my mom and dad, my sister Molly, my marriage and divorce, everything that has happened over the years. I think of Dr. Kislov and all my surgeries.

Julian of Norwich's words come to me: *All shall be well, and all shall be well, and all manner of thing shall be well.*

As the organ plays the first strains of "Amazing Grace," I open my mouth and sing.

Acknowledgments

There are many people who have been cheerleaders of this project over the years. My love and deep appreciation go to my champions and friends Fred Klein and the entire Puddingline, especially Susan Chiavelli, whose early suggestions resulted in the powerful braiding of the events in the first chapter.

To my archangels, Michael, Richard, Edmund and Tim, you made up the composite Michael in this story, but each of you in your own way saved my life. You will always be in my heart.

To my yoga teacher Sue Anne Parsons and all my yoga buddies, thank you and Namaste.

My deep gratitude also goes to my precious flamingo sisters, Ruth Thompson, Jayne Benjulian, Sandra Hunter, Tania Pryputniewicz, Lisa Rizzo, Barbara Rockman, Michel Wing and Barbara Yoder…trusted friends and writers who provided both encouragement and thoughtful insights that vastly improved this work.

My unending love, affection and thanks go to my cousin Maureen Fimpler and her husband, Bill, who opened their home to me every six months for two years so I could go back to school. Buckets of the same to my cousin Cheryl Ball (Maureen's sister) and her husband, David, who generously provided me an exquisite Costa Rican hideaway to finish my MFA thesis, which was the basis for this book.

And finally, deep warm fuzzies to Cathy Armstrong and Wendy Rockwood and all our now-departed canine companions, who made every day of my life a day at the beach.

A version of the chapter "Scar Tissue" was printed in *The Louisville Review* (Spring 2013) as "Jasmine Ghosts."

ABOUT THE AUTHOR

Marcia Meier is an award-winning writer, writing coach and developmental book editor.

Her other books include *Unmasked, Women Write About Sex and Intimacy After Fifty* (Weeping Willow Books, 2018), *Ireland, Place Out of Time* (Weeping Willow Books, 2017), *Heart on a Fence* (Weeping Willow Books, 2016), *Navigating the Rough Waters of Today's Publishing World, Critical Advice for Writers from Industry Insiders* (Quill  Driver Books, 2010), and *Santa Barbara, Paradise on the Pacific* (Longstreet Press, 1996).

A newspaper journalist for nearly twenty years, she has freelanced or written for numerous publications, including the *Los Angeles Times*, *The Writer* magazine, *Santa Barbara Magazine*, *Pacific Standard Magazine* and *The Huffington Post*.

She holds a bachelor's degree in journalism and an MFA in creative writing, and has taught writing at the collegiate level and in private workshops for more than twenty years.

Visit her at marciameier.com

CPSIA information can be obtained
at www.ICGtesting.com
Printed in the USA
JSHW021307160121
10916JS00002B/146